KT-539-575

THIRTEEN TIBETAN TANKAS

Tanka 1

COURTESY CITY ART MUSEUM OF ST. LOUIS

Gautama Buddha, with his two great disciples,
Śāriputra and Maudgalyāyana

EDNA BRYNER

Thirteen Tibetan Tankas

པོད་ཡུལ་གྱི་ཐང་ཀ་བཅུ་གསུམ་དག །

THE FALCON'S WING PRESS

The Tibetan inscription on the title page is the book title translated into Tibetan.

Die stamp on front cover of book: Gautama Buddha, from the first folio of the Ch'ien Lung Suvarṇaprabhāsottamasūtra manuscript.

Copyright 1956 by The Falcon's Wing Press, Indian Hills, Colorado. All rights reserved. This book or any portion thereof may not be reproduced in any form without written permission from the publisher, except for purposes of quotation in a review printed in a newspaper or magazine.

Library of Congress Catalogue Card No.: 55-11367

Manufactured in the United States of America

To Dr. Bernhard Geiger

BUT FOR WHOSE PENETRATING TEACHING,
INEXHAUSTIBLE PATIENCE, AND UNFAILING HELPFULNESS
THIS STUDY WOULD HARDLY HAVE BEEN MADE

Foreword

My association with the author of the present volume goes back to the year 1939, when she first came to me as a student, mainly interested in acquiring a thorough knowledge of Sanskrit and Tibetan, after she had become acquainted with the spiritual world of the East through translations such as *Sacred Books of the East*, edited by F. Max Müller. Her ambition at that time was personal rather than scientific: she wanted, for her own benefit, to gain an insight into the characteristic ideas and workings of the Eastern mind and hoped to get nearer the core of the matter by translating direct from the Sanskrit and Tibetan sources, in which so many of the sacred treasures of the East have been preserved.

As Sanskrit and Tibetan were not part of the program at the institution at which I was then teaching, I proposed to her to start with what I was offering—the study of Pahlavi—and afterward Avesta, through which she would become acquainted with the Zoroastrian religion. Accordingly, we devoted several semesters to extensive readings in the books of the Middle Persian Zoroastrian literature and in the Avesta, with special reference to the Gāthās of the prophet Zarathustra.

Meantime, we had proceeded to the classical modern Persian literature, beginning with Firdousī's Shāhnāma, the "Book of the Kings."

From there we went on to the works of Persian mysticism (Sūfism), as represented by the poets Ḥāfiz, Jalāl 'uddīn al-Rūmī, and Farīd 'uddīn 'Aṭṭār, including the biography of the great mystic Abū Saʿīd ibn abī 'l-Khayr. These studies in Iranian religion and philosophy created a valuable background.

Turning next to Sanskrit, the author was introduced to the study of the Vedas (in particular Rig-Veda and the Upanishads), the Sānkhya philosophy, the Bhagavadgītā, Patanjali's Yogasūtra, the Laws of Manu, and the Hitopadeśa. This was followed by extensive readings in the Pali Jatakas.

Then came Tibetan. Beginning with Jatakas from the Dzanglun, there followed Songs of Milarepa, the Life of Marpa, and work on a manuscript of the Bardo Thödol and parts of the Suvarṇaprabhāsottamasūtra.

It had long been in the author's mind to make a special study of her own translations of Tibetan Jatakas in connection with a new approach to the doctrine of rebirth, fundamental in Buddhistic belief. Fortunate in having volumes of the Kanjur placed at her disposal by generous owners of the Tibetan scriptures, she began intensive work on the Jatakas. While in the midst of this, she was asked by the Curator of the City Art Museum of St. Louis if she would make a study of the stories depicted on thirteen Tibetan tankas the museum had purchased. The present volume represents the results of this study, which extends much farther than was originally planned.

This first scholarly publication of the author's presents an important contribution in its identification of the scenes on these thirteen tankas with the stories of Ārya Śūra's Sanskrit poem *The Jātakamālā or Garland of Birth-Stories*.* It is rich in other historical information

---

* The Sanskrit text was edited by Hendrik Kern in the Harvard Oriental Series, Vol. I (Cambridge, Mass., 1891). It was translated into English by J. S. Speyer, in *Sacred Books of the Buddhists*, Vol. I (London, 1895).

that will undoubtedly prove highly interesting both to specialists in Sanskrit and Tibetan and to readers outside this sphere. I refer in particular to the beautiful paintings, masterpieces of Tibetan art, that illustrate the book, and to their descriptions by the author; to the birth-stories in Chapter II, told with artless simplicity and vividness; to the analyses of the content and format of Tibetan scriptures; and to the critical comparisons of different versions of the same story, especially the famous "Feeding the Tigress" story.

The author was confronted with hardships in reading manuscripts that were damaged in many places and often difficult to decipher. Her work gives evidence of a methodical approach to problems and of sound judgment. I am confident that this work will contribute significantly to the understanding of the idea of rebirth as contained in Sanskrit and Tibetan Buddhistic texts as well as to a deeper insight into folklore and Tibetan art portrayal of the Jatakas.

BERNHARD GEIGER

Columbia University
August 31, 1956

General Editor's Preface

T**HE** J**ATAKA** T**ALES** or Buddhist Birth Stories ("Birth-iana" would be the literal translation of the Sanskrit plural), whence the scenes of these tankas or banners—so ably described by Miss Bryner—are derived, have been told in almost every important language of the globe since pre-Christian times, and even in some tongues now no longer used, such as Sogdian. The stories appear to have arisen in India out of Hindu mythology, folklore, and religion (e.g., the Mahabharata) preceding the Buddhistic reformation of Brahminism that was to sweep through India and finally take root elsewhere to the north, south, and east. Our tankas represent but a small selection from a vast literature.

The tales, however, attained their fame in their Buddhistic form. The fables of Aesop are now known to have come from India, stemming from these same Buddhist tales. The famous Christianized version of one of the Jataka Tales appears in the well-known spiritual romance of *Barlaam and Josaphat* (the latter name being the final corruption, via Persian and Arabic, of the Buddhist title *Bodhisattva*, assigned to spiritual heroes).

This version, aside from its recension in the *Gesta Romanorum*—a source that is filled with Buddhist borrowings—is to be found in the Armenian, Syriac, Ethiopian, Arabic, Hebrew, Persian, Georgian, Greek, Latin, and West European languages. The earliest Western text of this ubiquitous Jataka Tale, as far as we now know, is that of Aristides in the time of Hadrian, now preserved only in Syriac, rather than the much later text of John of Damascus from the seventh century of the Christian era, believed before the work of J. A. Robinson in 1891 to be the oldest text of the Christianized adaptation.

Through Indian traders Jataka Tales have found their way to Africa, into Bantu folklore. The Ethiopian version of *Barlaam and Josaphat* mentioned above is not primarily an indigenously African adaptation of the Indian original, but is simply a Coptic Christian version. However, we find in Bantu native versions of the Sumsumara and Vedabbha Jatakas, to name two, the latter being also preserved in Chaucer's *Pardoner's Tale*.

Shakespeare is not immune from the Jatakas, as parts of *As You Like It, King John,* and *The Merchant of Venice*—including the famous pound of flesh—have been traced conclusively to their Buddhist forerunners. The diffusion of the Jataka Tales illustrates but one part of an even more fundamental and significant fact: the pervasive influence of Oriental upon Occidental culture, directly as well as by Hebrew, Greek, and later, Arabic transmission.

Like Ceinan, the lovely and royal daughter of Ceinwawr in Welsh Druidic legend, the face of truth in this matter of Oriental influence has been so overlaid with extraneous erroneous conceptions that she is no longer bright and fair. Our history, religion, and philosophy students are rarely allowed to guess from their instruction as to the depth and magnitude of the Oriental (including Egyptian) contribution to our so-called Græco-Hebrew-Roman civilization. Basic Egyptian, Indian, or Sumero-Babylonian elements in Pythagoras, Plato, Aristotle, or, for that matter, Thales, Heraclitus, and Anaximander, are mostly allowed to go unmentioned or are misleadingly reserved for scant or skeptical reference.

Thus Plato's plain references to technical astrology in *The Republic* and *Timaeus*—with all their important implications as to the dating and extent of Sumero-Babylonian influence in early Greece—are glozed over or entirely ignored in the vast majority of our commentaries. The fact of Buddhist emissaries in ancient Egypt is seldom if ever brought to the ken of the Occidental student, much less the fact that India's then steady cultural intercourse with China thus also admits of Chinese elements passing fairly directly into the ancient western world. Furthermore, ancient India, through now proven trade routes to and from the Indus Valley civilization, knew Sumero-Babylonia at first hand.

And, carrying the matter one step still farther east, there is sound evidence that the script of the now lost Pacific civilization—a script preserved only on a few remaining "speaking boards" found on Easter Island—was identical or at the very least closely akin to the script used in the Indus Valley some five milleniums ago. Despite A. Métraux's surprisingly vindictive as well as invalid diatribe attacking the fine pioneer work of de Hevesy, G. R. Hunter's exhaustive affirmative demonstration of the identity (London, 1934) was concurred in by no less a student of ancient scripts than Professor S. Langdon of Oxford. These are all vital facts bearing on the degree of the ancient unity of world culture, as traced through diffusion.

Returning from their far-reaching ramifications to the Jatakas themselves, we may appropriately recall the spirit of the Buddha, who in a past incarnation (as Sudashan, son of King Shivi, in the Sogdian version of the Vessantara Jataka) has just finished the purificatory washing of a Brahmin in a scene so reminiscent of the New Testament story of Jesus' washing his disciples. As Sudashan, the Bodhisattva then says (at the end of the 12th folio of the Sogdian MS):

O may I obtain Buddahood!
May I shut fast the gates of hell
And deliver thence the damned,
Leading them to the emancipation of Nirvana
By the same path that past Buddhas have trod.

C. A. MUSES

Indian Hills, Colorado
August 1956

Author's Preface

THE WORK presented here must be designated as exploratory. At least, that is what it was at the outset when I cast about—in the shadowy region of Jatakas, where the provocative subject of rebirth has tenacious roots—for light on what has kept rebirth fundamental in Buddhistic teaching. The region of Jatakas, in spite of their considerable number available in German, French, and English translations, is still somewhat like the remote forest where the fabulous Bodhisattva deer Śarabha lived his yoginlike existence—a forest "untrodden by travellers and showing nowhere any traces of vehicles or carriages, the tracks of whose feet or wheels might have beaten something like a road or border-line; yet, intersected with channels and full of anthills and holes."[1]

Jatakas are stories of former existences of the Buddha and those about him. The neglect of their proper cataloguing so as to make them readily discoverable throughout the 325 volumes of Tibetan scriptures was deplored by Léon Feer,[2] the translator into French of Alexander Csoma's analysis, in English, of the Kanjur and the Tanjur (the two collections of Tibetan scriptures).[3] In the face of the handicap noted by Feer, who was himself the translator of a number of Jatakas, I was plunged into a thicket of the Jataka region in being asked, fortuitously one might say, to identify twenty-nine birth-stories portrayed on thirteen Tibetan tankas belonging to the City Art Museum of St. Louis. That was the beginning of this work.

Ballasted, fortunately, by having already translated some fifty Jatakas from the Kanjur, after many false starts leading over innumerable ant-hills or into treacherous holes in the almost trackless territory, I came suddenly upon Ārya Śūra's great teaching collection, *The Jātakamālā or Garland of Birth-Stories,* translated from his Sanskrit into English by J. S. Speyer. This collection definitely placed the stories as pictured on the paintings. Here they all were, in order!

But where to find the translation from the Sanskrit into Tibetan? Hinted at, said to have been seen by someone somewhere, reported authoritatively to be in existence. Only when I was nearing the end of my work on the present volume did I find it, accurately catalogued—in the French Index to the Pekin edition of the Tanjur. This index, made by Dr. P. Cordier,[4] led to the finding of the Sanskrit-into-Tibetan in the Narthang edition, in Volume 91 of the mDo division. The only difference between the Pekin and the Narthang volumes is in the number of folios taken up by the Jātakamālā—152 folios in the former and 148 in the latter. Volume 91 of the mDo division of the Tanjur became accessible to me so short a time before the completion of this work that I was not able to do more than check the Sanskrit-into-Tibetan against Speyer's English translation of Śūra's Sanskrit. I found that the Tibetan rendering adhered closely to Śūra's original as trans-lated by Speyer.

The episodes of the scenes on the tankas have been identified with Śūra's stories. They are culled from Speyer's English version.

Among the birth-stories I had already translated from the Kanjur were several obviously to be taken as the original source material on which Śūra had patterned certain ones of his poetical teaching stories, handed down orally to his time. The words falling from the Buddha's own lips into the ears of his disciples, shaped to show up an "occasion" in the present as being the result of the inevitable working of the Law of cause and effect, convey strikingly the penetrating power of the Buddha over his disciples. His telling differs in many respects—in action, in wording, even in character presentation—from Śūra's, as the translations from the Kanjur in Chapter V show. What a task to look forward to, had one another lifetime at hand, to study each of the stories in Śūra's collection and ferret out the same story as originally told by the Buddha on the special "occasion" into which it fitted!

In the translations of the selected stories, I have attempted to keep the flavor of the Tibetan agglutinative language, which has a charm uniquely its own in causing to ring out at times deeply hidden layers of primitive feeling. A regular English translation tends to flatten out the Tibetan, which, with its many humpings and reversals—acrobatics even—is delightful to read in its own progression.

Prose and poetry are effectively combined in these stories. When a character speaks out his inner attitude, the heightening of his emotion is expressed in 7-, 9-, 11-, etc., syllable verses, four to a stanza. Instead of rhyme, there is strange, to our ears, rhythmic utterance, especially in sorrow, almost as if below human speech, in cadence with the mourning of animals or suffering vegetation. I have tried to convey this in translating verse, in spite of the difficulty of adjusting English to Tibetan syllables. It is hoped that the reader will bear with any seeming irregularities and roughnesses.

The Sanskrit and Tibetan words written in roman in this book—for example, nirvana, karma, mandala, chorten, sutra, guru, Upanishad, Jataka—are found in *Webster's New International Dictionary, Unabridged*. Such words as have not come into the English language have been italicized and given diacritical marks.

Many have had a part in this work. To Dr. Bernhard Geiger, to whom this book is dedicated, great thanks are given for having opened up to me, some years ago, a long-desired field of research and for having encouraged and helped me in every possible way to find what enabled me to undertake this work.

To Mr. and Mrs. Louis Horch, unbounded gratitude for having so generously loaned volumes of their Narthang Kanjur for a leisurely first study of the Jatakas. And to Mr. Fritz Ehrenfest, special thanks for bringing about the initial contact instrumental in providing such a rewarding experience.

To Dr. Thomas T. Hoopes, Curator of the City Art Museum of St. Louis, great gratitude for providing excellent photographs of tankas and inscriptions for the preliminary exploration, for sending the tankas to the Metropolitan Museum of Art in New York to be studied at leisure, and for unlimited encouragement and help all along the difficult way of presenting these paintings, one might say, on their own terms.

To Mr. Alan Priest, Curator of Far Eastern Art at the Metropolitan Museum, and to Mr. Aschwin Lippe, Associate Curator, heartfelt gratitude for providing ideal conditions for the examination of the tankas.

To Dr. Johannes Rahder, Professor of Japanese, Tibetan, and Mongolian Languages and Oriental Philosophy at Yale University, very special thanks for constant encouragement and for supplying references to informative and photographic material of great value, especially in relation to the "Feeding the Tigress" story.

To Mr. Wesley Needham, Curator and Cataloguer of the Lhasa Kanjur at Yale University, deep gratitude for his kind help in locating material in the Lhasa edition and for permission to reproduce the transfer impression shown in Plate I.

To His Reverence, Dilowa Hutukhtu, special thanks for help in deciphering a part of the Viśvantara inscription.

To Mr. S. Yudkoff, thanks for photographing Tankas A and B; the first and last folios of the Tibetan volume containing Ārya Śūra's

Jātakamālā; the three folios and board cover of the Suvarṇaprabhāsotta-masūtra; and the transfer impression.

To Mrs. Adele Garrett, a grateful tribute for editing and organizing the manuscript in a highly creative way, and for her perceptive questions that brought to light the need for further research on my part, which resulted in clearing up many difficult matters.

And finally, by the power of fate, *stes-dbang-gis,* as the Tibetans have it, to the late Count Stefan Colonna Walewski (whose *A System of Caucasian Yoga* was published by The Falcon's Wing Press, 1955) for suggesting a publisher for this work.

I am deeply grateful to the City Art Museum of St. Louis for supplying photographs of the thirteen tankas. For other illustrations I am indebted to the following: To the East Asiatic Library of Columbia University, for permission to photograph Figures 1 and 2 from a Tanjur volume; to Vanoest, Les Éditions d'Art et d'Histoire, for Figure 7, reproduced from *Histoire des Arts du Japon,* by Jean Buhot; to Dietrich Reimer, Berlin-Lichterfelde, for Figures 8 to 13, which are reproduced from *Die Buddhistische Spätantike,* by E. Walderschmidt; and to the Harvard University Press, for Figure 14, which is reproduced from *The Twin Pagodas of Zayton,* by Gustav Ecke and P. Demiéville. Thanks are also due to Harcourt, Brace and Company for permission to quote from *All and Everything,* by G. Gurdjieff; and to W. Heffer & Sons, Ltd., Cambridge, England, for permission to quote from *The Buddhism of Tibet,* by L. A. Waddell.

May *Thirteen Tibetan Tankas* cast a few tiny beams of light over the region of investigation first trekked out amid immense hardships by researchers such as Alexander Csoma de Körös, Sarat Chandra Das, R. Spence Hardy, W. Woodville Rockhill, and many others, to whom no words can express sufficient gratitude.

E. B.

Contents

Illustrations

In parentheses after each tanka number in the series
is the number of the tanka in the collection of
the City Art Museum of St. Louis.

Facing Page

ILLUSTRATIONS

Facing Page

ILLUSTRATIONS

Facing Page

Om! Adoration to all Buddhas and Bodhisattvas!

I

Tibetan Art and Teaching

THE THIRTEEN Tibetan tankas, or banners, presented here attest,
in their telescopic scenes from twenty-nine of the Buddha's many existences before he became the Great Being, the living quality of a vast
and mighty religious art. That art arose, some five hundred years before
Christ, out of the challenging teaching of the Perfectly Enlightened
One, Gautama, the Buddha, taken in and given out, century after century, in recurring waves of heart-lifting hopefulness. As it spread out
from the Master's native India, it carried the glorification of his earthly
path throughout the subtle complexity of nations comprising Central
Asia, until, some five hundred years after Christ, it brought its uni-
verse-embracing directive power to Tibet.

Amid ever multiplying influences, this religious art had undergone
a thousand years of intensification and of extended "speakingness"
(*brjod-pa*)—for that was its prime function—before it reached Tibet,
its new, high, and hard Himalayan home. There it came into its own
anew. It was as if Tibet had been preparing itself slowly, surely, over
the years, to develop a special genius in the blending of art and religion.

Our thirteen tankas demonstrate this in their setting forth of subject matter thoroughly known and sacredly dear to the heart of every Tibetan.

Gathering rich nourishment in its far journeying, that art came to Tibet, it is popularly claimed, by way of the two Buddhist wives of the country's famous King Srong-btsan-sgam-po. One, a Nepalese Princess (her marriage sealed an alliance between her father, King Amshuvarman of Nepal, and the Tibetan king) brought with her an array of Buddhist images, among which was Akṣobhya, one of the five Dhyāni Buddhas. The other Buddhist wife, Wen Ch'eng, a Chinese Imperial Princess (her marriage in A.D. 641 accented a peace treaty in which the T'ang Emperor T'ai-Tsung recognized the Tibetan king as supreme in Kuku-nor), brought a famous statue of the Buddha represented as a young prince.[1] Both of these precious depositories of power are now in the Jo-Khang in Lhasa, which King Srong-btsan established as his capital.

The king surely did not marry those princesses in order, as some have gone so far as to say, to get possession of the images. But it is authoritatively vouched for that he was enormously helped by both of them to spread the Doctrine, especially by his Chinese consort. In recognition of their helpfulness, the two ladies were "canonized" by the Buddhist church as incarnations—in the green and white aspects, respectively—of the divine Tārā, the Merciful, she who with compassion guides travelers across the infinite ocean of transmigration.

That King Srong-btsan was already a Buddhist seems conclusive in the light of Tibetan historical works, which affirm that Buddhism was at work in *Bod-yul* ("country of Bod," as Tibet is generally called) long before the advent of the princesses.[2] We have, indeed, an old account of an extraordinary preview of Buddhism in Tibet more than two centuries before the king married these princesses.

This old, authoritative account is found in the Introduction to

W. R. S. Ralston's *Tibetan Tales*, a translation into English from F. Anton von Schiefner's German translation (made in 1869) of the Tibetan original. It states that in the sixtieth year of the reign of King Lha-tho-tho-ri (he is said to have reigned one hundred years, A.D. 367-467), there one day descended from heaven upon the golden terrace of his palace "namely, the image of two hands in the position of prayer, a golden pyramid-temple (*chaitya*) an ell high, a small coffer with a gem (*cintāmaṇi*, 'wish-granting jewel') marked with the six fundamental syllables (*om maṇi padme hūṃ*),"[3] and a copy of the Kāraṇḍavyūha *sūtra* (religious dissertation), presumably from Nepal, since that country, not China or India, venerated this sutra especially. Not understanding the nature of the holy objects, King Lha-tho-tho-ri ordered them to be locked up in his treasury. While they lay there, "misfortune came upon the king," in the way of children being born blind, failure of fruits and grain, cattle plague, pestilence. After forty years, there came five strangers, supposedly missionaries from Nepal, to the king. They asked him how he could let such mystic and powerful objects be cast into the treasury, presumably explained them, and suddenly disappeared. The king then ordered the objects to be brought forth, to be attached to the points of standards, and to be treated with the utmost reverence. After that, all went well, with children, fruits, cattle.

No doubt a good deal must have happened, in the way of Buddhist influx, in the two hundred years between the dramatic preview and the momentous marriages. The very first concern of King Srong-btsan, on coming to the throne, was to form an alphabet for the Tibetan language, there being as yet no written characters but the use, instead, of "stick-writing" (notched pieces of wood) and "string-talk" (knotted cordelettes) for communication and documentation.[4] For this purpose, several years before his first marriage, the king sent seven nobles to India. Unable to find a way there, they returned without having accomplished anything.

Undiscouraged, the king then dispatched, with sixteen talented companions, the gifted Thon-mi Sambhota, who, having reached southern India, learned the Indian characters from a Brahman and a Pandit. Afterward, becoming acquainted with the handsome Devanāgarī Sanskrit alphabet, in use at that time in Kashmir, Thon-mi devised out of it the highly decorative Tibetan, which shows to such advantage amid the scenes on many Tibetan banners. Thon-mi also translated many sutras before returning to Tibet, among them the Kāraṇḍavyūha, a copy of which had fallen from heaven two centuries before on King Lha-tho-tho-ri's palace terrace. He carried back with him, too, a large collection of religious works.

King Srong-btsan soon became proficient in the use of the new alphabet, and he was credited with much Buddhist translation. Thus he was well prepared to marry Buddhist wives.

The descending of Tibetan searchers for an alphabet and for the Doctrine into the Buddha's land stirred Buddhist missionaries into toiling up through the plains of India over old trade routes and along precipitous trails across Western Tibet. The missionaries brought with them arrays of sacred images, which firmly embedded Indian artistic tradition as basic in the development of Tibetan art. The iconography, for the most part, goes back to the Greco-Buddhist Gandhara school of northwest India, in which the Buddha is represented as a human being. These images, used doubtless then as today to illustrate teaching or preaching, presented principally the Great Being himself, the chief Bodhisattvas (that is, saints who had attained the highest station next to the Buddha), and scenes from the Buddha's life—not only from his life as the Buddha, with its so frequently pictured four greatest events and four greatest miracles, but also from his former existences as he himself told of them to the Brotherhood.

And so, thirteen hundred years after India's religious art and teaching had come to Tibet, we find ourselves in a museum in America—

the City Art Museum of St. Louis—before thirteen inimitable Tibetan tankas. In the center of each sits the Buddha, Perfectly Enlightened, Completely Liberated, free to leave this earthly life forever or compassionately to reincarnate in order to help others still struggling on the way, as he, in the little scenes surrounding him, is shown struggling in former existences in varying forms and levels of being, as king of men or of geese, as lord high treasurer, as majestic white elephant, as baby quail.

⚘

Tankas, the most characteristic product of the whole Tibetan painting field, are not a spontaneous creation of Tibetan talent but a type of painting borrowed from India. In time they received the imprint of Tibetan genius. The Indian models, called *paṭa*, are, as Giuseppe Tucci explains in his monumental work titled *Tibetan Painted Scrolls*,[5] of three types:

1. Tissues painted with images and symbols of divinities, used for magic or as work producing merit. There was no greater merit than to diffuse, by any means whatever, the Buddha's teachings, thus enlightening souls in darkness and permitting those who merely look upon the painted images to accumulate good *karma*. (In Buddhism, *karma* is the doctrine of consequences, the working of the law of cause and effect. That is, a person's acts in one existence determine the rebirth level in his subsequent existences, in unending succession, until, by continuous effort, he has freed himself.)

2. The mandala, a projection of the cosmos for the purpose of evoking deities. It was originally drawn upon the ground and erased after the performance of the rites, just as the American Indians of today make their sand paintings.

3. Painted representations of the lives of saints, for the use of storytellers and guides to holy places.

Our tankas fall into the third category.

The word *thang* means a plain, or flat country. *Thang-ka*, or *thang-sku*, is an "image, properly of human beings; at present equals picture, painting, in a general sense, also of landscapes, etc."[6] The word *thang-ka*, which stresses the formal aspect of the picture of an image, has taken the place of *ras-bris*, or *ras-ri-mo* ("design on cotton"), which stresses the material. Tankas are hung in immense numbers in temples and private homes; borne in religious processions; and carried into lonely places by wandering lamas to serve in their preaching. To all who see them, tankas keep reiterating the "hope of ultimate deliverance of every living thing, subhuman, human, and superhuman."

We are indeed fortunate to have in the series presented here such worthy examples on which to center our attention.

The date of these paintings? Invariably, this is the first question asked by the Westerner, with his addiction to dates. Well, certainly after the seventh century A.D., probably along the way toward the twentieth. If we could see perhaps two thousand such paintings, we might possibly place them in order within these thirteen centuries. Long journeying in time and far in space lies behind them. The banners, bearing their little scenes of daily life, in different color tones and arrangement, proclaim the at-one-ment of all life in its ever recurring, ever varying, same scenes. Tibetan artists do not date their work, nor do they (one high period was an exception) sign their names. They remain anonymous, out of time and space, working in the eternal verity NOW, while producing sacred images that have power.

This power aspect may have something to do with the fact that (as stated in George Roerich's *Tibetan Paintings*) a Tibetan who owns a tanka will hardly part with it, especially if it is consecrated by some high lama and has an imprint of the lama's hand on the reverse side. A non-Buddhist outsider has no chance at all of acquiring such a tanka. Most of the paintings found in Western public and private collections have been thrown on the market because of wars and upheavals that destroyed lamaseries and impoverished rich painting-possessing families.

The thirteen tankas of the present volume's title came from the famous von Staël-Holstein Tibetan Art Collection, lately sold, after the great collector's death, in America. Two supplementary tankas, illustrated in Chapter V, have been designated as Tankas A and B. I bought them from the New York dealer who had sent the thirteen to a St. Louis dealer for the City Art Museum's consideration. In the St. Louis set, two tankas are missing, but Tankas A and B are not the missing ones. They belong to another, though similar, set. Both sets were painted to present the teaching stories of the Buddhist poet Ārya Śūra.

Art in Tibet is entirely religious. Tibetan methods and atmosphere of work in art are very much like religious art work in former centuries in all countries, such as in Early Renaissance Italy or Old Russia. The youth who desires to be an artist does not go to an art school to learn his craft but goes to a master, living with him, as do a certain number of other pupils, and helping him with his work. In the big centers of religious life, such as Lhasa, there are any number of painters. The Dalai Lama and the Tashi Lama always have a great staff. The Tibetan artist, moreover, never stays long in one place, but travels about, doing murals in some monastery or sacred pictures for the chapel of a wealthy family. He goes to far-distant places, where he learns new things from local activities and gives of his own in return. This makes for great similarity of art products in the various provinces and resultant difficulty in determining their origin.[7]

A tanka is usually painted on silk or cotton. The thirteen tankas in the St. Louis series are on cotton. The material is stretched on a frame and then covered with a thick mixture of glue and chalk, which must be polished evenly with the smooth surface of a conch. The production of the painting proceeds very slowly. Everything must be drawn according to canonical rules: First the principal figures, predominantly the Buddha or Bodhisattva, are drawn. The face is preferably drawn on auspicious prescribed dates, usually on the fifteenth day of any month, and it is colored on the thirtieth day, these two dates being held sacred. Then the surroundings are drawn in—sky, hills, waterfalls, ponds, houses. The most minute details of ornamentation must be completely worked out before the coloring begins.

In making the design, Tibetan artists often use a transfer method—as do the Russian icon makers—for the various sacred images, in order that the required iconographic details may be canonically correct. There are so many of these details that a draftsman would have to be enormously knowing to sketch an image freehand correctly. In such places as Derge (a province in Eastern Tibet), there are collections of these transfer impressions, called *tshags-par*, or "dotted impression," outlined in red or black ink but not giving the coloring of the images themselves.

A transfer impression outline from Derge is illustrated in Plate I. This woodcut places Marpa (central figure), the first of the Tibetan gurus ("Teachers") of the Kargyütpa School of Northern Buddhism, in his apostolic line. The line begins (top center) with "Dorje-Chang, the 'Holder of the Dorje' (the Spiritual Thunderbolt of the Gods), in Whom the Esoteric Lore of the Kargyütpas has its origin. The Established Church regards Him as an Emanation of the Buddha Shakya Muni" (top left corner). It also "venerates Him, as the Kargyütpas do, as the Chief of the Celestial Buddhas, analogous to the Ādi, or Primordial, Buddha of the Old School of Padma Sambhava." (The quoted parts are from Evans-Wentz's *Tibet's Great Yogī Milarepa*, in which he describes "The Great Kargyütpa Gurus.")

Robed in princely attire, with "passive mien" and "beautiful countenance," Marpa sits enthroned in the Buddha pose on a lion-throne. "The bell in His left hand symbolizes the Voidness as Intellect; the dorje in His right hand symbolizes the Divine Method and Spiritual Power." His blue color, his necklace of bone-beads, all the details of

PLATE I

This woodcut of a transfer impression shows the Tibetan method of painting sacred images when they are not drawn freehand. The artist transfers a dotted impression to his canvas by means of a needle, then outlines it in red or black ink, after which all details are worked out in color. The woodcut is from Derge, a district in Eastern Tibet.

presentation (Evans-Wentz describes them as iconographically belonging to "Him") give some idea of the richness that the painter is invited to bring forth in his coloring.

On the right of the Celestial Buddha is Tilopa, the first of the human gurus, an Indian yogi, who received direct guidance and teaching from the Celestial Buddha. Tilopa holds aloft in his right hand a golden fish, symbolizing "sentient beings immersed in the Ocean of Worldly Existence"; and in his left hand a blood-filled skull, symbolizing his ability to confer occult powers pertaining to the world.

Opposite Tilopa is his favored disciple, Naropa, the second of the human gurus. He is blowing a trumpet made of a ram's horn, proclaiming the glory of his Order. Naropa was a professor of philosophy in the celebrated Buddhist University of Nālanda, in northwest India, the principal center of learning of that epoch. It was there that Marpa, on one of his manuscript-collecting journeys to India, met Naropa and became one of his disciples.

Marpa made a number of journeys to India for manuscripts, which he translated from Sanskrit into Tibetan, thus becoming known in Tibet, his native land, as Marpa the Translator. Famous in the line of Kargyütpa gurus, he nevertheless did not renounce family life and so is represented here in the semi-lay dress of a native Tibetan of good family.

In India, Marpa also met Atīsha (top right corner), an Indian Buddhist monk, from whom he obtained special teaching. Atīsha went to Tibet in A.D. 1038 and became the first of the Reformers of Lamaism, introducing celibacy and higher morality among the priesthood.

Milarepa (lower left corner), A.D. 1052-1135, Marpa's uniquely great disciple, sits, supposedly, in a cave on an antelope skin.

Gampopa (lower right corner), A.D. 1077-1152, Dvagpo-Lharje— that is, Physician of the Dvagpo Province (in Eastern Tibet)—was Milarepa's most spiritually gifted disciple, from whom "onwards to our own day the Kargyütpa Dynasty of Teachers has continued without a break." He is shown in the garb of a lama, supposedly on a richly embroidered cushion in a preaching booth.

All the figures offer the artist a wealth of opportunity to work out in color the iconographic details belonging to each figure.[8]

The Tibetan artist, in using the transfer method, lays the impression on the surface on which the painting is to be done and goes over it in outline with a needle. Then he traces the needled outline in red or black ink—an operation that is sometimes performed by an advanced student. The result is bound to be a more or less rigid design, but the rich coloring, with its immense possibilities of ornamentation, as done by the master, gives the high mark to the painting.

The predominant colors (mineral, rarely vegetable), according to Tucci, "are lime white, red, yellow (obtained from arsenic), green (from vitriol), vermillion (from carmine), blue (from lapis lazuli), and indigo. Mineral colors are pounded in a special stone mortar with a wooden pestle. Gold is much used for backgrounds and ornaments; the use of silver is rarer."

Tucci asks whether we should consider Tibetan painting as "nothing but the production of a class of craftsmen living on a perfunctory tradition," and then answers his question by reflecting on Tibetan art of the eighteenth century: "The artist says neither more nor less than what he feels: he gives himself up to his images, and they obediently settle on canvas, with the levity, even with the haziness, of things seen in a dream."

On the subject of the images, Tucci quotes from an older source: " 'The image, all of whose lines are complete, is a bestower of happiness, while the image in which they are lacking causes all sorts of evils.' (Vivaraṇī, ed. H. Mitra, p. 1.)" The painter does not copy nature. He follows prescribed "measurements of perfect creatures. But this perfection, we repeat it, is not the perfection of an ideal beauty, it is the expression of an inner superiority, the manifestation, through signs and proportions, of a nature transcending humanity, the symbol of participation in an essence different from that which common creatures are made of."[9]

It is expressly laid down canonically in the Kanjur—one of the two big collections of Buddhist scriptures which early searchers brought from India and to which they added commentary—that the artist must be a saintly man of good behavior, learned in the scriptures, reserved in manner; and his place of work must be clean and proper for the making of sacred images. Usually he is a lama, knowing thoroughly the traditional teaching. He accompanies his work with continuous reciting of prayers. Sometimes another lama is present, who reads prayers aloud while the artist works sitting on the ground, holding the painting on his knees. Round him, his disciples prepare colors and attend to his needs, with advanced students sometimes coloring the outlines of figures drawn by the master.

Those who have seen the making of sand paintings by American Indians—so well demonstrated at the Museum of Modern Art in New York in 1941—have observed an atmosphere of work similar to that of tanka-making in Tibet. The Big One, long versed in his tribe's esoteric lore, draws the design and fills in the center work, while his helpers grind the colored rock and hand him the tiny bags of sand as he needs them. After a while, the best helpers are brought in to carry on as the Big One directs, and finally the second-best helpers do the details of edges. These sand paintings of the American Indians, like the mandalas in old India, are made and erased in one day. Tibetan tankas, on the other hand, whether presenting mandalas or birth-stories, are produced for permanence. The tankas must withstand long and hard use in being put up and taken down in temples and home chapels and in being borne in processions.

The finished painted surface, called *me-long* ("mirror"), is framed on all sides by woven material, usually silk. Tucci finds that the frame makes the picture all the more impressive, and he accounts for the symbolism of characteristic parts of the borders of tankas:

> The frame, by a skillful succession of tones, in harmony with the colors of the painting, seems to guide the eye, through ably graded shades, to a maturer enjoyment of the picture.
>
> Besides the frame proper, the painting is usually enclosed by two bands, also of silk often yellow or red; they are called 'ja' dmar, ser "red, yellow rainbow" and, according to their name, they symbolize the rainbow as a celestial light irradiating from the image, to signify that the painting is a reflection of remote heavens, diffusing a divine radiance.
>
> On the inferior border is often applied, exactly in the center, a square piece of silk stuff of another color and more prized. Tibetans call it t'an sgo, "door of the tanka."
>
> Not infrequently, indeed whenever it is possible, this applied patch or the space corresponding to it on the silken band, is wrought with figures of dragons. This may seem simply a decorative pattern, but it answers to an exact symbolism: it represents the sphere of cosmic waters, of the endless and inexhaustible possibilities which are latent in the world of maya, the "becoming" contrasted with the planes of spiritual purity represented in the painting: on one side intellect, on the other nature and matter.[10]

The bottom edge of the tanka is pasted on a bamboo rod. The ends of the rod are often carved in the shape of flowers. The banner *must* be rolled upward: it is a desecration to roll it from the top down.

❁

Painters, it is said, guard their own secret tenaciously. The artist of each of our thirteen tankas (or artists, for usually, according to Roerich, a draftsman does the drawing and a painter the coloring, one producer seldom being found in whom both talents are equally developed) must have had a rich secret. And the artists surely sketched the scenes on the tankas freehand, so very supple were they in their handling of the iconographic images they had to use. This became all the more patent to me when I came across a tanka bearing scenes of the first ten of the stories depicted on Tankas 1 to 4. In this banner that I saw by chance, the placement of the figures, in coloring bright and naïvely decorative, is simply a stiff scattering, with no real design.

In our banners, the unimpeachable balance of aesthetic form is like a straightforward declaration of belief in the lovely lotus-enthroned Buddha figure in the center, round which, as state of Perfection, the striving, whether of man or animal, moves. "Just as, brethren, a dark blue lotus or a white lotus, born in the water, comes to full growth in the water, rises to the surface and stands unspotted by the water, even so, brethren, the Tathāgata (having been born in this world), having come to full growth in the world, passing beyond the world, abides unspotted by the world."[11]

The lotus throne, according to Tucci, symbolizes (1) "creation as a whole . . . within time and space"; and (2) "the sign of the 'other plane' revealing itself in the center of the inner space, in the heart."[12] The expanse of the heart space is defined in the Chāndogya Upanishad: "As far, verily, as this world-space extends, so far extends the space within the heart. . . . What is within that, should be searched out."[13]

On our banners, the searching for what is within the heart space is suggested in the way the scenes of the little stories, beginning at the bottom of each banner, mount upward in artful turning, with Sakra (Indra), the Lord of the Thirty-three Devas, usually somewhere near the top, sensitive to the heating of his throne from the vibrations of some high work the Bodhisattva is performing. Sakra is ready, in his fear that the Eminent Struggling One will get the throne away from him, to trip him in his striving. Sophistication toward the events of daily life and a tender sharing of them are subtly displayed in the rich, ever varying shades of pastel blues and greens, reds and yellows, together with generous amounts of gold that make a shimmering surface atmosphere.

Witness the adroitly free manner of placing more than fifty figures on Tanka 12, bearing scenes from two Jatakas (birth-stories). At the bottom is the Bodhisattva as the Great White Elephant, in five attitudes: meeting the lost strangers and telling them what to do; climbing the cliff above the watering place to which he has directed them by a different, easy way; on top of the cliff, ready for his plunge downward in sacrifice; the plunge itself; his dead body being used, as he had counseled, for food and for skins in which to carry water for the rest of the journey. Above is the story of King Sutasoma (the Bodhisattva), who converted the cannibal: letting himself be seized, while at his bath, by the whirling human-flesh-eater and being carried up the cliff to the dreadful bone-strewn retreat; winning his release to go to fulfill his pledge to the old Brahman; returning again to the final struggle in which he accomplishes another step up the ascent toward Buddhahood.

❀

"OM! ADORATION TO ALL BUDDHAS AND BODHISATTVAS!

"Grand and glorious, of inexhaustible praise and charm, comprising excellent virtues and thereby auspicious, are the wonderful exploits which the Muni performed in previous births. Them will I devoutly worship with the handful of flowers of my poem.

" 'By those praiseworthy deeds the way is taught that is leading to Buddhahood; they are the landmarks on that way. Further, even the hard-hearted may be softened by them. The holy stories may also obtain a greater attractiveness.' So I considered, and for the benefit of men the attempt will be made to find a favorable audience for my own genius, by treating of the extraordinary facts of the Highest One in the world in a manner which is in accordance with the course of facts as recorded by Scripture and Tradition.

"Him, whose beautiful practice of virtues, while acting for the sake of others, no one could imitate, though bent on self-interest; Him, the blaze of whose glory is involved in his true name of the All-Knowing

One; Him, the Incomparable One, together with the Law and the Congregation I venerate with bowed head."[14]

Thus the great Buddhist poet, Ārya Śūra, introduces his *Jātakamālā or Garland of Birth-Stories*. Twenty-nine of his thirty-four tales (two tankas in the St. Louis series are lacking, presumably bearing the other five tales) are portrayed on our thirteen paintings. Śūra's work, written in purest Sanskrit, was discovered by Brian H. Hodgson[15] about 1828, when an old Patan monk showed it to him among other interesting Buddhistic writings. Mr. Hodgson procured copies of it. "Perhaps the most perfect writing of its kind," its English translator, J. S. Speyer, pronounces it, with its skillful managing of artful prose and verse displaying great ingenuity in the "handling of a variety of meters some of which are rarely to be met with elsewhere."

Who was Ārya Śūra? Speyer states that he was a Buddhist Teacher (the word "Teacher" is equivalent to the Sanskrit *guru*) and man of letters who "must have lived before 434 A.D."[16] Winternitz, in *A History of Indian Literature*, says that Śūra "probably belongs to the fourth century A.D.," and that "among the frescoes of the caves of Ajanta there are illustrations to the *Jātakamālā* with verses by Ārya Śūra in inscriptions."[17] F. Max Müller cites a statement by Tāranātha, historian of Tibetan Buddhism, to the effect that Ārya Śūra composed the *Jātakamālā* at the end of his life, when he was corresponding with a certain king, Kanika (Kanishka?).[18] Waddell, in *The Buddhism of Tibet*, states that Kanishka was a Scythian king of northern India, under whose auspices an epoch-making council was held at Jalandhar toward the end of the first century A.D.[19] The council, according to Waddell, established a permanent schism in Buddhism and affirmed the superiority of the Mahayana system; this, however, is much disputed. In *The Blue Annals*, Kanishka is mentioned as a "king from the country of Uttarapatha."[20]

Ārya Śūra was known by many names, according to Tāranātha. One name was Ashvaghosha, a contemporary of Kanishka's. However, among all the names cited by this historian, there is only one—Mātṛceṭa —that seems to proffer a possible, indeed probable, alter idem, according to D. R. Shackleton Bailey (translator of Mātṛceṭa's "Hymn of 150 Verses"),[21] who found resemblances in meter, vocabulary, and phraseology between the "Hymn" and Śūra's "Garland."

In manuscripts the poet's name is given as Ārya Śūra. This name is corroborated by Chinese tradition, by the Chinese translation from the Sanskrit of the *Jātakamālā* bearing his name on the title page, and by Tibetan tradition, which reveals him to have been famous as a Teacher and transmitter of birth-stories. (It is this *Jātakamālā* that Speyer translated, and it is from his translation, with its appropriate, lofty phrasing, that the stories told in Chapter II have been adapted.) The woodcut image on the first folio of the Tibetan translation of the *Jātakamālā* in the Tanjur,[22] even shows Śūra on the right end—balancing the Highest of the Buddhas on the left end. This Tibetan translation was made by Vidyākarasiṃha, of India, and Mañjuśrīvarman (corrector), who followed the Sanskrit, apparently faithfully, as revealed by Speyer's English.

Ārya Śūra selected, from the traditional store of more than five hundred birth-stories, some so well known that he often did not even give names to his characters. He set out to write a hundred Jatakas showing how the Buddha acquired the ten *Pāramitās* ("means of getting to the other side"): giving, moral practice, self-abnegation, wisdom, exertion, patience, truth, resolution, good will, equanimity. For each Great Perfection, Śūra allowed ten stories. But he died on completing only thirty-four.

Śūra's masterly text is solidly embedded in Tibetan Buddhistic history. It was handed down from century to century through other great, and lesser, Teachers and scholars, who learned from those qualified to pass on the provocative stories and taught in their turn. No doubt, they were well served by just such illustrating tankas as those shown in the frontispiece and Plates II to XV.

A passing glance at some of the outstanding ones among these Teachers and scholars may mirror for us something of the sort of person Śūra himself must have been. Five, from the eleventh to the fifteenth centuries, are named in *The Blue Annals, the Stages of the Appearance of the Doctrine and Preachers in the Land of Tibet*—one of the two main sources of information for all later historical compilations concerning the "Land of the Snows." (The other main source is *History of Buddhism*, by Bu-ston Rin-po-che, composed A.D. 1322.)

The first Teacher mentioned is Po-ta-ba Rin-chen gsal (A.D. 1031-1105). Having practiced meditation until the age of 50, he thereafter labored for the benefit of others. Followed constantly by more than a thousand disciples, he assiduously preached Śūra's *Jātakamālā* as one of the "Six Basic" Texts of the *bKa-gdams gzhung-drug* ("six kernel," or "main substance," instructions) so that the "High-sounding name of the 'bKa-gdams' became famous during his time."[23]

Another was the great scholar and translator, sTengs-pa lo-tsā-ba Tshul-khrims 'byung-gnas (A.D. 1107-90). At the age of six, already worthy of historical notation, he "peeped through a hole in the Wall and saw numerous countries (filled) with caityas. Later, when he came to India, he discovered it to (be the same country seen previously by him)." At 10, he was able to cure the ailments of others by blowing on them. At 15, ordained as a monk, he copied volumes of scripture in order to get means to go to India, "without regard for his life." Studying extensively under thirteen scholars, translating and revising existing translations, among them Śūra's *Jātakamālā*, he became one "whose benefit was great for the Lineage of the Recitation of the Sūtras in Tibet."[24]

Still another great Teacher was gYag-sde pan-chen (A.D. 1299-1378). He began to study the Doctrine at the age of five, attending in all on 108 Teachers, learning the many texts he was to hand on—especially, the *Jātakamālā*—and becoming, "since he possessed the faculty of prescience, one able to labour extensively for the welfare of others."[25]

Dharmasvāmin Nam-mkha dpal-bzang-po (A.D. 1333-79), son of an almsgiver, showed, from the age of five, great commiseration for the sufferings of others. He was ordained at seven, and at eight the faculty of prescience was born in him. At 11, he remembered his former existences in India, gTsang, and other places. Later, perceiving also his future existences when in meditation, he attributed his quick development in this life to having practiced meditation for a long time in gTsang. At 18, he learned the *Jātakamālā*, able at that time to know by heart complete texts heard but once and to recite them perfectly to others.[26]

"Now the Great Translator bSod-nams rgya-mtsho (A.D. 1424-82): In the garland of his former existences, he performed the labours of the three boundless accumulations.

"For the welfare of living beings, he reached the end of the Path. Though he had attained the Highest Enlightenment (Abhisambodhi), a state characterized by renunciation and knowledge which cannot be improved upon, there is no doubt that he had assumed the form of a Mahāsattva, a leader, who strove to convey the travellers-disciples to the firm ground of salvation."[27]

He took rebirth "as the equal of ordinary living beings in the eyes of his disciples" until he appeared in an uninterrupted succession of scholars and saints (*siddhas*). His father had miraculous powers; his mother was a natural *ḍākinī* (literally, "sky-goer"; Tibetan *mkha-'gro-ma*, "wise" women of supernatural powers, represented sometimes like angels, or fairies, or witches).[28] Accompanied by miraculous signs before and at his birth, he performed, at the age of four or five, extraordinary deeds, such as salutations and making offerings to the sacred images at bSam-yas (monastery); preaching to his playmates on the suffering of this Phenomenal Existence; composing a beautiful poem, perfect in words and meaning, for his mother, who was fond of poetry; dwelling in mystic trances, in which he had countless visions.

"Brought up with special veneration in the midst of an ocean of plenty," bSod-nams rgya-mtsho became "like a lotus in a lake, the nectar of the eyes of all peoples." He was ordained at seven or so, and at 13 was preaching the great Prajnaparamita. From that age onward, he proceeded on his destined path of a great scholar in the learning of sutras and tantras, among them the *Jātakamālā* as one of the "Six Basic" Texts; in the mastering of various sciences, such as prosody, medicine, the arts; and in gaining knowledge of rites and tantric methods, such as ritual dancing, songs, and the drawing and outlining of mandalas.

Acquiring, at the age of 22, the virtues of an ordained monk, he went ever on into higher development—opening the gates of knowledge by reflection, acquiring beatitude through the power of the Buddha's blessing, attaining the degree of a fully enlightened Mahāsattva, and having power over the miracle of rebirth according to his own desire.[29]

❀

No wonder the birth-stories are known to every Tibetan. They thread their golden way down through the ages. Forceful tongues delivered them to receptive ears. The stories retained the "lure for feeling" challenging the artist to his particular expression of what has been painted innumerable times. They constitute the "other side" of the paintings, loading them with a wealth of lore. Without some knowledge of this lore, it would be difficult to take in the implications of the pictured representations.

There is always an "occasion" on which the Master tells the story of his former existences. Something has happened in which the Buddha and some of his disciples have been involved, as when Devadatta, his archenemy, plots to have the king's savage elephant maddened by drink and let loose in the street through which the Buddha is destined to go, hoping thus to bring about his death. Ānanda, the Master's most beloved disciple, puts himself in the way of the elephant three times to save his Master. But the Master, pushing Ānanda back three times, performs a miracle—one of the four great miracles so often pictured from the life of the Buddha—in which he subdues the elephant and on the spot teaches him the Law.

The Brotherhood, gathered together afterward in their own domain, must speak perforce of how Ānanda was ready to sacrifice himself for the Master. The Master, in his "perfumed chamber," knowing intuitively that they speak of Ānanda's merits, comes forth, asking, though he already knows, what they discuss. On their answering, he says: "Not now only, but formerly, Ānanda, even when he was born in animal form, was ready to renounce his life for my sake."

He then tells "a story of the past"—so beautifully pictured on Tanka 10—when he lived as Dhritarāshtra, leader of a great flock of golden geese, on Lake Manasarowar, with a commander-in-chief, Sumukha by name (now Ānanda). These two know "not other business than that of supporting the body of Salvation for their flock of geese." Brahmadatta, at that time King at Benares, hearing constantly in his council of the Holy Goose King and his wonderful helper, had his councilors advise him how to allure them. Thus, a beautiful lake was constructed in a forest near the city, and proclamation was made daily that security would be given to all birds coming there. Two of the Holy Goose King's subjects, happening to fly that way and seeing the beauty of the lake, reported it to their king, who, in spite of his worthy commander-in-chief's attempts to dissuade him, led his great flock to the lake. As Dhritarāshtra alighted there, in his golden splendor, with his magnificent companion, a clever fowler watched them. This fowler, Nishāda by name (now Buddha's disciple Channa), was commissioned to catch them.

What delicacy there is in the picturing of the snare that Nishāda made, fit only for its Golden Captive, with its artless looping against the ground and the curving out of its dainty hooks, secured at both ends with a golden pin!

In the snare, the Bohisattva caught his foot, but in spite of pain from the injury he did not utter the "cry of dangerousness" until his flock had finished eating and so, well fed, could fly away in a great hurry. Meanwhile the fowler had drawn near. Sumukha, who had remained with his Master, begged to be taken in place of his Lord. So in admiration was Nishāda of such faithfulness, that he finally consented. Then Sumukha said: "But take us both, free and unbound, to your king, and no doubt he will reward you exceedingly." Nishāda granted his request. The king, after having heard the whole story of the faithfulness, rewarded the fowler and, paying great respect to both the Holy Geese, released them. Afterward the Golden King returned and preached the Law to King Brahmadatta.

"I do not think that the imagination of any race," says the French Indianist Alfred Foucher, "has ever created a finer or vaster subject for a poem than this destiny of a single being in whom are shown all the aspects of life, in whom is concentrated all the experience of past ages—in one word, in whom the evolution of the entire race is reflected."[30]

It is the *wholeness* of the process of being born again and again, no matter in what walk or even form of life, striving each time for greater perfection or perfection in another aspect of being—in contrast to the process of being born as a man striving to go to heaven and avoid hell—that would seem to offer the great hopefulness of an endless scale of values, the immense joy of *being alive more and more*. An ever recurring new possibility of this kind would, in its energetic impetus toward thrusting forth into expression, blossom out into just such an art as the Tibetans developed.

Our thirteen tankas are *teaching* paintings, and they go deeply into the matter of birth successions. "Arising from the moral legends speaking of the Bodhisattva," is the way the inscription for Tanka 2 introduces the whole series of birth successions. Similarly, the picturing of the lives of the saints of the early Christian church taught what it meant to endure the hardships of life in such a way as to obtain sainthood. That the Christian church had the doctrine of rebirth until A.D. 553, when it was banned by the Council of Constantinople,[31] a fact not commonly known, is something to ponder on.

In Buddhistic belief, nothing happens by chance. What one enjoys or suffers on earth now is the result of his own deeds in former lives, along with the deeds of his fellow beings. One pays off old debts or enjoys the fruits of former lives, or both. Whatever good he does on earth now is placed to his account for a future life on earth. This is karma. The world is one system in which nothing is ever lost. When all debts are paid, when the accumulation of virtue completes the being, one is liberated: a Buddha.

Ordinary people do not remember their past existences. Highly enlightened beings, such as Pythagoras (according to tradition), do remember. There is a stage of development at which it is possible for many persons to do so. "In India, this recollection of previous lives is a common feature in the histories of the saints and heroes of sacred tradition,"[32] says Cowell in the Preface to *The Jātaka or Stories of the Buddha's Former Births*. Such recollection is mentioned by Manu as "the effect of a self-denying and pious life."[33]

Whether the Buddha (or anyone else) was actually, or only symbolically, born in previous existences as an animal has remained a source of argument throughout the ages.[34]

A presentation that throws light on the subject of karma and rebirth is found in *All and Everything*,[35] by the late George Gurdjieff, in which he elucidates how "higher-being-bodies," or "souls," began to arise in our Universe. His exposition is briefly set forth in the following paragraphs:

Man is not born with a soul; he is born only with the possibility of making a soul. He is born with a first-being-body, called "planetary," which is composed of cosmic crystallizations that originate on the planet Earth, come from it, and ultimately return to it. "Dust to dust." He exists as an animal until he makes of himself something more than an animal; and this he does by "conscious labor and intentional suffering."

By conscious efforts he can build a second-being-body, which is composed of substances transformed by the sun and by planets other than the Earth. The degree of development to which this second body rises depends on what a man has done with his life. If he has done nothing beyond existing as an animal, then the second-being-body is not formed and there is nothing to survive. But if he has made efforts toward an aim higher than and beyond himself, the second body he makes becomes the vehicle for making his third body, the "higher-being-body," the real part of man on which the hopes of his Creator were placed. This higher-being-body, because it is formed of substances arising from the Sun Absolute itself, cannot be destroyed by any process operating in the rest of the universe. It is the body of true immortality and is capable of further self-perfection. This is the Buddha body.

At death, the second and third bodies go together into the sphere from whose cosmic substances the second body had its arising. There, after a time, the second body dies. If the higher part of this second body has not yet arrived at the state of "objective Reason," it must find a "similar-two-natured-arising-corresponding-to-itself" into whose second body it may enter when the perfected third body of that "two-natured-arising" is in the act of departing. There it continues its further perfection.

In this "exchange-of-the-external-part-of-the-soul," as Gurdjieff calls it, may lie the source for the being-born-again-as-an-animal notion called "metempsychosis."

This, in effect, might well represent the process underlying the

Buddha's progression through an untold number of previous existences to his high state of perfection—that of "an independent individual with its own individual Reason."

Whether or not some such process was esoterically taught to highly developed disciples would be known only to initiates. On our thirteen tankas are portrayed twenty-nine of the Buddha's former existences in what may be considered exoteric terms understandable to the great mass of aspirants toward perfection.

❀

On each tanka the picturing always begins at the bottom and mounts artfully upward. So, on Tanka 2, the story about the tigress begins in the lower left corner, with the Bodhisattva sitting in his forest retreat, teaching all who come to him, before he starts off with a disciple to the plateau region where he sees the starving young mother and gives his body to her. The second story on this tanka starts at the lower right with the bestowal of gifts by the excessively charitable King of the Śibis. Other scenes of giving carry the story up and across the banner to the top, where an old blind Brahman (Sakra) asks for and gets one and then the other of the king's eyes; then over to the right, where the blind king sits beside the lotus pond and Sakra appears to him, gives back his eyes, and adds gifts of further seeing. At the top, right corner, in beautiful balance to the tigress scene, is the giving of food portions by the King of Kosala, aided by the queen in this giving.

In similar movement and flow of scenes, the other tankas give a pictorial rendering of Śūra's teaching.

II

Stories of Scenes on the Tankas

Oᴜʀ sᴇʀɪᴇs of paintings begins with a presentation of the Buddha in his human aspect as created by the Gandhara school. (See Tanka 1, frontispiece.) He is seated on his lotus throne, attended by his two venerable disciples, Śāriputra and Maudgalyāyana, who appear many times along with him in events in his former existences. Monastic in appearance, without ornaments, he is portrayed here, as on almost all the banners, in his reddish-brown robe, thrown over both shoulders, his uncovered chest disclosing his golden body. He has the protuberance Ushnisha on the skull, and the sign Urna between his eyebrows. With his right arm extended down to the edge of the throne, he makes the sign of attestation with his hand. On the palm of his left hand, which is on his lap, he displays a design of the Wheel of the Law. Below the throne is an altar bearing the Wheel of the Law and offerings. Farther down is the Corpulent Wealth God, Kuvera, with his special emblem, the lemon, and with his mongoose spewing out jewels. At the top, center, is the Garuda bird (*khyung*), with golden wings, biting a serpent (*nāga*). At top left is the future Buddha, Maitreya; and at top right, a Dhyāni Buddha.

The presentation of the Buddha is the central tanka in the City Art Museum of St. Louis series. The twelve other tankas are supposed to be arranged in a definite order, six to the right and six to the left of this central one. These twelve tankas present Ārya Śūra's birth-stories as indicated by inscriptions in cursive Tibetan pasted on the back of the tankas—in the sequence given by Śūra. Unlike inscriptions in block print, used frequently as part of the painting itself, these are written in the so-called "headless" letters used for manuscripts and in cursive work.

In the present chapter the stories portrayed by the scenes on the tankas are told in summation from Speyer's English translation of Ārya Śūra's *Jātakamālā*. They have been checked sufficiently with the Tibetan translation of Śūra's Sanskrit to make sure of a satisfying conformity.

A considerable number of these stories are also found in *The Jātaka or Stories of the Buddha's Former Births* (edited by E. B. Cowell), a collection from the Pali comprising 547 Jatakas, told with a wealth of detail and with more folklore than moral emphasis. The Pali, a vernacular language developed as early as 250 B.C., became a literary language and, in the words of Mrs. Rhys Davids, "was the vehicle of what is, so far as we have yet been able to discover, the earliest formulated records of Buddhism."[1] According to F. Max Müller, tradition has it that the Jatakas composed in Pali "were taken to Ceylon by Mahinda, about 250 B.C., that the commentary was there translated into Singhalese, and that the commentary was retranslated into Pali by Buddhaghosa, in the fifth century A.D. It is in this commentary alone that the text of the Jatakas has come down to us."[2]

For those stories in Śūra's *Jātakamālā* that are also found in the collection from the Pali, see the "Notes" section at the end of the present volume, which gives the number of the Pali story corresponding to the Śūra story. (The Pali numbers are taken from E. B. Cowell's *The Jātaka or Stories of the Buddha's Former Births*.)

Tanka 2

Arising from the moral legends speaking of the Bodhisattva (*byang-chub-sems-dpai rtogs-pa brjod-pa-las byung-ba*)

First birth succession, giving (his) body to a tigress (*stag-mor lus sbyin-pai skyes rabs-te dang-po*)

Born in an eminent and mighty family of Brahmans, the Bodhisattva took no delight in the wealth, distinction, and fame that fell to his share as the result of merits formerly earned. Retiring to a region of plateaus, he became a hermit, teaching any who came to him. One day, accompanied by a disciple, he went on up to more solitary regions, for meditation, where he saw a young tigress, so hungry that she was about to devour her newly born young ones. Sending his disciple off to look for food for the starving mother, he cast his body down from a precipice, attracting the attention of the tigress, who at once began to eat this "manna from heaven." The disciple, returning without any food, found the dead body of his Master and ran weeping to his companions, while the remains of the Bodhisattva were strewed from heaven with a rain of garlands.[3]

Second birth succession, as King of Śibi country (*yul-śi-bi-pai rgyal-por skyes rabs-te gnyis-pa*)

The Bodhisattva, as King in the Land of the Śibis, was distinguished by all virtues, but especially the virtue of charity. Not satisfied with giving away riches only, he conceived a desire to offer his own body. From this desire of his, the earth trembled. Sakra (Indra), Lord of the

Devas, remarked this; and, always ready to test anyone desirous of great-deed-doing, went in the form of an old blind Brahman to tempt the king, begging for one of his eyes. "Has someone instigated you?" asked the king. The Brahman replied that Indra had instructed him.

In spite of attempts by his ministers to dissuade him, the king gave first one eye, which, by a miracle performed by Indra, adhered to the eye of the Brahman. The king then tore out his other eye, giving it in the same way. After some time, Indra appeared to the king, who was sitting on the bank of a pond in his park, and offered him whatever he wished, but the king did not ask for anything. This brought about the coming back of both the king's eyes. The earth trembled, the sea overflowed, great phenomena were beheld. And Indra, since he had been unable to persuade the king to ask for a single boon, gave further to him the ability to see one hundred leagues in every direction, then disappeared. The king returned to his people and delivered a sermon on being liberal.[4]

Third birth succession, is as giving a portion of warm food (*zan dron tshangs-pa phul-bar skyes-pai rabs-te gsum-pa-o*)

The first (ones) of the 34 birth successions (*skyes rabs so bzhii dang-po*)

The Bodhisattva was King of Kosala, pious, charitable. One day he remembered his last previous existence. Greatly moved, bestowing generous gifts, he spoke two stanzas about what he had done before. No one understood the stanzas. On the queen's asking him to explain them, he said that formerly, having been a slave in that same city, he had given four sramanas, who had asked for alms, a small dish of gruel, accompanied by pious thoughts. "Out of that sprout" had sprung "this tree of greatness." Then the queen, urged by the king to recall her former birth, remembered herself as a servant, who had fed a hermit,

Tanka 2

Feeding the tigress
Giving up his eyes
Presenting food portions

PLATE II

COURTESY CITY ART MUSEUM OF ST. LOUIS

PLATE III

COURTESY CITY ART MUSEUM OF ST. LOUIS

Tanka 3

Filling an alms bowl
Grass-cutting for the needy
Burned-body offering

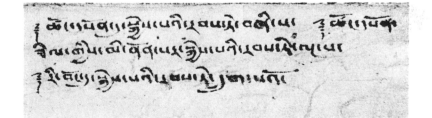

for which act she was now a queen. There followed a little sermon in praise of charity.[5]

Tanka 3

Fourth birth succession, as head of a guild (*tshong-dpon-du skyes-pai rabs-te bzhi-pa*)

The Bodhisattava, a rich and pious merchant, had just had a fine meal served up when a Pratyekabuddha came, placing himself in the gateway of the house with his alms bowl. (Lower left corner of banner, across to right, and up halfway.) Māra, the Wicked One, wishing to hinder the act of charity, caused a deep flaming hell to arise between the mendicant and the threshold of the house. The merchant sent his wife to proffer abundant alms, but in fright she returned to him. Then he himself went. He saw the awful hell, with Māra coming out of the house wall in divine shape to stand in the air, trying to dissuade him from charity. The Bodhisattva, however, knowing Māra, boldly stepped into the fire, in the place of which, because of his virtue, lotuses suddenly appeared. He handed the food to the Pratyekabuddha, who, to show satisfaction, flew up into the air, while Māra, discountenanced, disappeared into hell.[6]

Fifth birth succession, as Avishahya, One-Unsurpassed-in-Splendor (*tshong-dpon zil-gyis mi non-par skyes-pai rabs-te lnga-pa*)

The Bodhisattva, born of an illustrious family, became the head of a guild. He was so affluent as to appear to be another Kuvera. He distinguished himself by such boundless generosity as to attract the attention of Sakra, the Lord of the Devas, who, wishing to try him, caused all his goods, little by little, to disappear until at last there remained only a sickle and a coil of rope. Not to be thwarted in continuing his giving, the Bodhisattva earned his living by weeding out grass, selling it, and giving what he could to the needy (left center of banner). Overcome with admiration, Sakra appeared to him, still trying to tempt him away from giving. The Bodhisattva did not succumb, where-upon Sakra restored his wealth, asked pardon of him, and disappeared on the spot.[7]

Sixth birth succession, is as a hare (*ri-bong-du skyes-pai rabs-te drug-pa-o*)

"The practice of charity according to their power by the Great-minded, even when in the state of beasts, is a demonstrated fact. Who, then, being a man, should not be charitable?"

The Bodhisattva was born as a hare in a forest region frequented by ascetics. With him, because of his excellent qualities, lived an otter, a jackal, and an ape, to all of whom he taught the Law. (Top left of banner and across to right.) On one occasion the hare observed from the state of the moon that it would be full on the next day, and con-sequently it would be the feast of *poshadha* ("sabbath"), on which they must be ready to satisfy the wants of possible guests. The hare began to ponder what he was to do, for he could not offer to guests the blades of grass that he cut off with his sharp teeth. He decided to offer himself. From his resolve, the whole of nature became agitated. Sakra, remarking it, went to try the hare, showing himself in the shape of a hungry old Brahman, crying as one lost and worn out from not eating. The four animals came to his rescue, the otter bringing his offering of seven fishes forgotten by some fisherman; the jackal, a lizard and a dish of milk; the ape, mango fruits. The hare offered his body. Sakra refused it, but afforded the hare an opportunity to give it by creating a magic bed of coals. On that fire the hare threw himself but was not burned. Sakra reverted to his lordly shape, praised the hare, and carried him to the moon as its embellishment. The other three were reborn in the world of the Devas.[8]

Tanka 4

Seventh birth succession, as Agastya (*Agastar skyes-pai rabs-te bdun-pa*)

The Bodhisattva, born of an illustrious family of Brahmans, enhanced its splendor and purity by his boundless charity from rich gifts that he was always receiving. Finally he cast away all that he had to become a hermit. The fame of his virtue, however, attracted many people, so that, in order to become completely detached from the world, he went to the island of Kārā, in solitude, offering to such guests as came roots and fruits, with fresh water, while he himself subsisted on what the guests left.

Sakra, Lord of the Devas, desiring to test his constancy, caused the roots and fruits that were fit for food of ascetics to disappear in that region. The Bodhisattva merely dressed young leaves on the fire for food, and continued his meditations. Then Sakra stripped the leaves from all the trees, shrubs, grasses. The Bodhisattva, taking such fallen leaves as were still good, boiled them in water and ate them. Sakra then assumed the form of a Brahman and came as guest to the Great Being, who bestowed upon him the whole of his boiled leaves, this being the Agnihotra sacrifice day. On five days successively, Sakra appeared and was fed on the Great Being's food. On his asking Agastya why he had undertaken such penance, the hermit replied that he wished to be freed from the wheel of births.

Seeing that the Bodhisattva did not covet his throne, Sakra offered him boon after boon. Having asked for riddance from covetousness and from innate evil passions, hatred, and fools, the hermit finally begged Sakra as highest boon not to come to him again in his blazing splendor, for fear it might turn him from fulfillment of penance. Thereupon Sakra bowed to him, circumambulated him, and disappeared on the spot, leaving behind him, however, to appear at dawn, plenty of divine food and drink with hundreds of Pratyekabuddhas to eat it and Devas to wait on them.[9] (This story takes up the lower half of the banner.)

Eighth birth succession, as Maitrībala, One-Having-the-Power-of-Kindness
(*byams-pai stobs-kyi skyes-pai rabs-te brgyad-pa*)

The Bodhisattva was born as a king, Maitrībala, righteous, pious, charitable. Once there entered into his kingdom five yakshas (*ojohāra's,* "taking away one's force"), who had been expelled by their lord, Kuvera, because of some transgression. Notwithstanding all their efforts, they were unable to rob even one inhabitant of his force, thanks to the king's virtues.

They saw in a forest a shepherd sitting under a tree, singing merrily. (The scenes begin, to the right of center of banner, with the encounter with the shepherd, and weave to the top, left, and over to the right.) Assuming the shape of Brahmans, they approached him and asked why he had no fear in such a lonely place. He answered that there was nothing to fear, because in the land was protection for all men in the form of their King Maitrībala, whom he counseled them to visit. This they did, asking the king for food. When he served them excellent food, they rejected it, saying they ate only human flesh. Then they assumed again their yaksha form. Against his ministers' attempts to dissuade him, the king had the royal physicians open five of his veins, from which he gave his blood to the yakshas to drink until they had quenched their thirst. Then, with his own sword, he cut pieces of flesh from his limbs for them to eat. Astonished, they asked him why he did all that for them. "To free the world from the wheel of births," he replied. Begging him to pardon them, they then promised not to destroy living beings any longer, and disappeared, whereupon the whole world rejoiced. Sakra, appearing with magic medicaments, healed the king.

Tanka 4

Proffering the last leaf (food)
Own flesh-and-blood bestowal

PLATE IV

COURTESY CITY ART MUSEUM OF ST. LOUIS

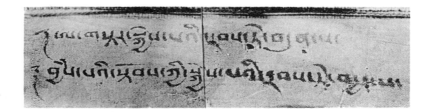

PLATE V

COURTESY CITY ART MUSEUM OF ST. LOUIS

Tanka 5

Exiled for excessive giving

Tanka 5

[Ninth birth succession, but the inscription does not state this.] Because Viśvan-tara, son of the King of the Śibis, offered as gift to a Brahman the most excellent elephant, the Śibi people were not pleased (*yul śi-bi-pa-rnams-kyi rgyal-poi sras thams-cad-sgrol-gyis bram-ze zhig-la glang-po-che mchog sbyin-par bcal-bai rkyen-gyi śi-bi-pa-rnams mi 'dod-du gyur-te*)

Viśvantara, together with Madrī and their young ones, Jāli and Krishṇājina, carried on their shoulders, entering on the footpath and . . . then the two children returned home . . . , entering into rulership . . . here . . . (*thams-cad-sgrol madri dang bcas gzhon-nu dra-ba-can kri-shna-'dzi-na gnyis-po pang-du thogs-te rkang-pai lam-du zhugs-pai par dang . . . de-nas sras 2 khor-nas rgyal-srid-du bcug-te . . . odir . . .*)

The Bodhisattva was born as the son of the mighty King of the Śibis, virtuous, just. As heir apparent, Viśvantara by name, the son was resplendent with every talent and virtue, and he was distinguished for extraordinary charity. On feast days, he rode about on his far-famed white elephant to inspect the alms halls where, according to his orders, the needy were fed. A neighboring king, wishing to have this white elephant, sent his Brahmans to beg it of the prince. At once he gave it.

The Śibi people, irritated at this excess of generosity toward for-eigners, demanded that the prince be exiled as not fit to ascend the throne. The king was compelled to consent. The prince, having dis-tributed all his wealth, willingly departed toward the penance-forest with his wife Madrī and their two children, Jāli and Krishṇājina. They were followed by a throng of people, whom the prince with difficulty persuaded to return. On the way some Brahmans asked for his horses. He gave them, and was ready to put on the yoke himself. But red deer appeared to draw the cart. Again a Brahman appeared; he asked for the cart itself. The prince gave it; and, taking his son on his shoulder, proceeded along the footpath with Madrī, who carried the daughter, to the penance-forest, where they settled in a hut constructed there by Sakra's orders. (The scenes begin at the bottom, picturing the family house and the alms halls where gifts are being handed out. Just below the central Buddha figure is the giving away of the white elephant. In the upper half the exiles get away to the penance-forest, after bidding farewell to parent, at right center.)

Tanka 6

(The other) half of the birth succession of Viśvantara and . . . (*thams-cad-sgrol-gyi skyes rabs phyed dang . . .*)

The story of Viśvantara on Tanka 5 continues on this tanka, with the prince watching over the children while Madrī was absent gathering fruits. A Brahman, whose wife had sent him, came to ask for a servant, and begged to have the prince's children for that purpose. The prince asked him to await the return of the mother, that she might take leave of them. But the Brahman did not consent. The prince argued that such little children would not be good as servants and counseled the Brahman to go to their grandfather, King of the Śibis, who would surely gladly ransom them. Again, the Brahman refused. The prince then handed over the children, pouring water, according to custom, over the Brahman's hand, in token of willing giving. The children begged to wait for their mother, but the Brahman took them away. He bound them with a creeper plant, from which they alternately escaped, hiding behind bushes, only to be caught and dragged onward.

Madrī returned and, disquieted on not seeing the children, asked questions of her husband, who did not give answers. She swooned. The prince, bringing her to, told her of his act of giving, of which she now entirely approved. The earth trembled from the effect of such high virtue. To finish the trial, Sakra went to Viśvantara in the shape of a Brahman, demanding his wife. The prince gave her, with her full assent, with the customary pouring on of water as a seal of willingness. The

Brahman then returned to his own form as Sakra, gave Madrī back, prophesied that both the children and the kingdom would be returned to the prince, and disappeared. This same Brahman, by the power of Sakra, brought the children to their grandfather, who ransomed them, pardoned his son, and fetched him and Madrī from the penance-forest.[10] (The scenes occupy the lower half of the banner.)

For a complete portrayal of this story, see the full translation and Tanka B in Chapter V. Whereas the Viśvantara story is divided in the St. Louis series between Tankas 5 and 6, it is presented as a whole on Tanka B. There is considerable variation in the presentation of the same scenes. (The progression of scenes on Tanka B begins, at bottom right, with scene of giving. Center bottom, Viśvantara and Madrī are in their home with the two children. Left corner, Viśvantara gives white elephant to Brahman, who takes it away. Scenes progress up the left side: the exiles start out in cart drawn by horses; the Brahman asks for and is given horses; Indra replaces them with red deer; the Brahman asks for cart and takes it away. Halfway up left side, the exiles begin their way on foot, with the children held on their shoulders. Above, Viśvantara is in his hermitage with the two children; the Brahman comes to beg them and takes them away. Top left corner, Madrī, out gathering roots and fruits, is stopped by the lioness on her way home. Just below, Indra, in Brahman disguise, asks for, and is given, Madrī. Top center, all is resolved with the elephant brought back and Viśvantara and Madrī returned to the kingdom, where the children have already been restored to their grandfather, the king. Down the right side are scenes of renewed giving.)

Of all the tales of the Buddha's former births, the Viśvantara story is the favorite. It is the tale of the last existence in which he is a Bodhisattva, before he becomes the Buddha, and represents the climax of the virtuous practice of charity. It is also the favorite of all the sacred plays with Southern Buddhists, according to Waddell, who, in *The*

Buddhism of Tibet, gave an abstract of a play being performed (at the time he wrote the book) in Western Tibet by a company of actors from Shigatse, in southeastern Tibet.[11]

Tenth birth succession, is as One-Making-Sacrifice (*mchod-sbyin byed-pai skyes-pai rabs-te bcu-pa-o*)

The Bodhisattva was a king, having reached this state as the effect of merit. He was a great almsgiver, behaving, indeed, like a Muni, knowing that people set a high value on imitating the behavior of the highest. There came a drought into his country. The king, ascribing it to his own or to his people's sins, consulted his councilors and Brahmans. They urged him to offer a Great Sacrifice of many hundreds of human beings.

The compassionate king, growing thoughtful, considered how to proceed. Finally he called the Brahmans and proposed a sacrifice of one thousand men. The Brahmans were content but feared a revolt of the people. The king stated that he would manage it so that the people would remain quiet. He ordered it to be proclaimed that he would sacrifice one thousand men, but only such as were wrongdoers. Every day an announcement was made that well-behaved people would not be molested but all evildoers would be seized for the royal sacrifice. At the same time, the king caused refuges for the poor to be erected everywhere. All now lived rightly, having from the king wherewithal to eat well, dress properly, and enjoy festival days. Then rain fell. The earth began to bear fruit, and abundance returned. The councilors eulogized the king.[12] (Across the top of the banner, from right to left and back again.)

Eleventh birth succession, as Sakra, Lord of the Devas. [The tanka presumably portraying the eleventh and twelfth successions is lacking. This would be Tanka 7 if the series were complete to the number of 15, as indicated by the inscription on Tanka 13 in the St. Louis series.]

Having practiced meritorious actions for a long time, and having come to possess "charity, self-restraint, continence, and compassion, directing his performances for the benefit of others," as Sakra, the Bodhisattva was ruling heaven and earth with a "glory which pervaded the whole universe." However, those spirits of darkness called Daityas ("demons"; "Titans"), unable to endure his renown and the wonderful bliss he enjoyed, drew up in battle array against him an enormous army of elephants, horses, chariots, footmen, and horsemen, with awful noise as of the wild ocean and such glitter of weapons that one could hardly look upon them.

In spite of his high level of righteousness, the Bodhisattva was moved to the frenzy of fighting because of the pride of his enemies, the danger to his own men, the regard for his majesty, and the traditional line of politically wise conduct. He mounted his thousand-horsed golden chariot, brilliant with precious stones and jewels, flaming with sharp-pointed weapons, and bearing a high-floating banner with an emblem on it of a figure in the attire of an Arhant (one-who-has-become-worthy, from *arh-*, "to be worthy"; highest of Buddhist saints). Leading his immense "divine host of different arms, elephants, chariots, horses, and foot," he met the Titans on the border line of the ocean.

A great battle ensued. Toward the end, Sakra's army began to take flight in terror of the great fiery missiles of the Titans. Only the Lord of Celestials held the field, barring the enemy host with his chariot. When the charioteer, Mātali, saw that the Titan army was about to be victorious and that the Deva army was on the point of fleeing, he turned the chariot toward retreat, but while it was ascending from the ocean border toward the Deva heaven, Sakra caught sight of some eagle nests in a silk-cotton tree—in the exact line of the chariot pole, which was about to ruin the nests. "The nests on that tree have young ones not yet winged," he said to Mātali. "Drive in such a way that they will not be crushed by the chariot pole." On Mātali's saying that he would have to turn the chariot and thus be overtaken by the Titans, Sakra ordered him nonetheless to avoid those nests, saying that it would be better to die by Titan club-strokes than live dishonored for having murdered those terror-stricken creatures.

The Titans, seeing the chariot turning, became panic-stricken, and their ranks gave way. The sight of the enemy's broken ranks made the Devas turn about from fleeing to pursuing, and they conquered the Titans. Verily, "Dharma in truth watches him who walks in righteousness (*dharma*)."

Twelfth birth succession, as a Brahman

The Bodhisattva, it is said, once came to life in an illustrious Brahman family, whose members were highly respected because of their ancestry and their righteous conduct. He received the various sacraments in due order. He lived at the home of his teacher, a learned Brahman, distinguished by birth and by practice of the customary conduct. The young man's quickness in learning the Vedic texts, his devoted obedience, his tranquillity, unusual in a youth, made his teacher love him dearly.

At intervals of rest from study, the teacher was accustomed to tell his disciples, in order to test their morals, of his own suffering from poverty, with no help from his family, no holiday-making, only wretched alms-begging. Much moved, his pupils did their best to bring him more and better food from their daily begging. He told them not to exert themselves in this manner, since it would not diminish poverty for any-one. Instead, if they could not bear his hardship, they should try to get wealth. Wealth, they replied, was not got by begging—their only means—since the people in that place were not very charitable. There were other ways of getting money, their teacher said (leading them on), as explained in law books. He himself, being old, could not put them into effect. "But *our* strength is not impaired by old age,

Tanka 6

Accomplishing perfection of giving
Making the great sacrifice

PLATE VI

COURTESY CITY ART MUSEUM OF ST. LOUIS

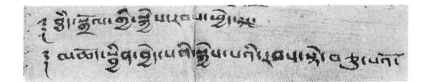

PLATE VII
COURTESY CITY ART MUSEUM OF ST. LOUIS

Tanka 7

Renouncing One-Who-Makes-Mad

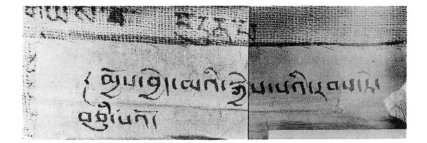

Master," the pupils replied; if he would inform them, they could put those ways into effect. No, he countered, young men's minds were too loose to carry out such resolution. Nevertheless, if they urged him, he would teach them one expedient. Theft, he advanced, was approved of for Brahmans in time of distress. Poverty, he supposed, was extreme distress. Moreover, it was no sin to enjoy others' wealth, since, indeed, the whole of those goods really belonged to the Brahmans (a sly twisting of the law). Only, he cautioned, no violence should be used, since that would harm their reputations. They should choose lonely places and times.

All approved except the Bodhisattva, whose innate goodness compelled him to oppose such advice at once, even though the others accepted it as a duty. Ashamed to look at his teacher, he remained silent except for gently sighing. Now the teacher, who had a high regard for that pupil's virtue, reflected whether the Great Being lacked courage or really knew theft to be wicked. "Speak, noble Brahman," he said. "Those twice-born men, incapable of bearing my misfortune, are willing to resort to the course of life followed by the energetic and the heroes; but in you I find nothing but indolence and dullness. You know my suffering. Notwithstanding this, you are keeping quiet!"

Troubled, the Bodhisattva saluted his teacher, replying that he did not lack affection, nor was he unmoved by his teacher's suffering. "But I think the mode of acting which my master has shown us cannot be put into practice" because "it is impossible to commit a wicked action without being seen." Nor did there "exist anything like loneliness" anywhere in the world for the evildoer. Always, "Invisible Beings and the purified Munis, whose eye is endowed with divine power," behold men's actions. The fool does not see them, thinking he is alone, and he sins. As for a lonely place, he knew of none; for, even if he saw no one where he was, that place was not empty of his own Self. His own Self witnessed the evil, being "more sharp-sighted than another person." Nor could he believe that his teacher would deceive them in this way for the sake of getting money. "As to my own determination . . . better is it to take the alms bowl and vile garments, beholding the opulence of the mansions of one's enemies, than to bend one's mind shamelessly to the murder of Righteousness, be it even with the goal of attaining the Sovereignty of the Devas!"

Rapt with joy, the teacher arose, embraced him, and lauded him with "Well said, my son! This is becoming to your keen intellect, adorned by tranquillity. My labor is crowned by success."[13]

Tanka 7

Thirteenth birth succession, having to do with the Intoxicated-Making-Woman (*myos-byed-mai skyes-pai rabs-te bcum*)

The Bodhisattva was King of the Śibis, "behaving like embodied Righteousness and Discipline, and being intent on promoting the welfare of his subjects like a father."

Now, in the capital of that king, one of the prominent townsmen had a daughter of such extraordinary beauty that she fascinated the eyes of all who beheld her and thus was called, by her relatives, Unmād-ayantī, "She Who Makes Mad." The father informed the king of having such a daughter, that he might take her as wife or renounce her. The king sent expert Brahmans to see if she had the auspicious marks for being a suitable wife for him. On seeing her, so struck were they by her beauty that they had no power over themselves. (The whole lower half of the banner shows the Brahmans examining her.) Fearing that the king, too, would be powerless because of her beauty and thus neglect his kingdom, they declared to him that the girl had inauspicious signs; and he renounced her. Her father then married her to one Abhi-pāraga, minister to that very king.

On a festival day, the king, while making a tour of the town to see the splendor of the festivities (right and left of center on the banner), passed near the house of his minister, to the roof of which Unmāda-yantī, angry that she had been spurned by the king, had ascended so that he would have to look upon her. He looked and, amazed at her beauty, asked his coachman who she was (upper half of banner, showing Un-mādayantī on the roof, to the right). On hearing that she was the wife of another, he went away and soon began to grow thin and wan.

The cause of his grief was discovered by his minister, who there-upon presented himself to the king (at the top, left), saying that a yaksha had disclosed the situation to him. He offered his beautiful wife to the king, who declined, declaring it a sin. Though the minister kept on trying in every way to persuade him, the king remained firm. The minister praised his constancy to the highest.[14] (In non-Buddhistic re-dactions, the king at last dies from love and the minister kills himself.)

Tanka 8

Fourteenth birth succession, as One-Arriving-Properly-on-the-Other-Side (*legs-par pha-rol-du phyin-pai skyes-pai rabs 14-pa*)

The Bodhisattva was born as an extremely clever steersman, Supār-aga by name, living in the seaport Supāraga. So "skilled was he in the art of taking a ship out and bringing it home" that, even in his old age, sea traders applied to him for his aid.

There once came merchants from Bharukkha, begging him to con-duct their ship on its trafficking. At first he excused himself on account of his blindness and age, but finally he consented. Having gone a long way, they met a great storm, which carried them far on into seas where there appeared strange fishes, resembling men, with ugly noses like a quadruped's hoof. Supāraga said they were indeed fishes, and this was the sea of Khuramālin ("wearing hoof-garlands"), and he advised them to turn back. No matter how hard they tried, they could not veer the ship about. So they went on through other strange and terrifying seas until they arrived in the sea Vaḍavāmukha ("mare-mouth"), where, indeed, destruction now threatened them. Supāraga, however, turned the ship about by an Act of Truth, declaring that he had never deprived a living being of life. In each sea through which they passed, he advised the merchants to draw up sand and stones, with which to charge the ship. It took them only one night, after having turned about, to reach the home port of Bharukakkha, where they found the ship full of jewels instead of sand and stones.[15] (Whole lower half of banner.)

Fifteenth birth succession, is as a fish (nyai skyes-pai rabs-te bco lnga-pa-o)

The Bodhisattva was born as king of fishes living in a certain small, beautiful lake, "wholly given up to the business of procuring for others what would be good and agreeable to them, even in this fish-existence. By the power of long practice, actions good or wicked become inherent in mankind to such an extent that they will perform them in a new existence without any effort, and, as it were, while sleeping."

It once happened that no rain fell for a long time, the lake began to dry up, and birds collected round the lake to eat the fishes. Seeing this, the Bodhisattva prayed for rain, relying on the Power of Truth that he had never done harm to any living being. Abundant rain began to fall, the birds flew away, the fishes began to recover, and the Bodhisattva, filled with joy, kept calling for the continuance of the rain. Sakra, Lord of the Devas, heard him and appeared, congratulated him on his virtuous power, and promised that never again should that lake, being the abode of his virtue, lack water.[16] (Right and left of center on banner.)

Tanka 8

Steering the ship properly
Rain-bringing by truth
Stopping oncoming flames
Preaching about a jar

PLATE VIII

COURTESY CITY ART MUSEUM OF ST. LOUIS

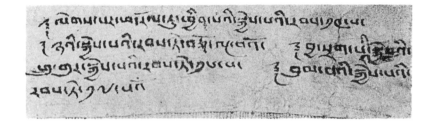

PLATE IX

COURTESY CITY ART MUSEUM OF ST. LOUIS

Tanka 9

Steadfast renouncing
Lotus-stalks theft
Upholding high opinion

Sixteenth birth succession, as a young quail (*bya-srag-pai skyes-pai phru-gur skyes-pai rabs-te 16-pa*)

The Bodhisattva was born as a young quail, living in a nest in the forest. When his parents brought living food, he did not eat it but ate only berries and seeds. He was therefore small and weak-winged, while his brothers grew up strong. Once a great conflagration took place, not far from the nest. The frightened quails flew away, leaving the little one who from weakness could not fly. When the fire was about to seize upon the nest, he addressed it, pointing out his helpless condition and himself as not being worth seizing, and begging it to stop. The fire did so, and up until today if fire comes near that spot it stops just there.[17] (Above the figure of the Buddha, to the right.)

Seventeenth birth succession, is about a jar (*bum-bai skyes-pai rabs-te 17-pa-o*)

The Bodhisattva was born as Sakra, Lord of the Devas. One day, in casting his eyes over the world of men, with compassionate feelings, he saw King Sarvamitra, given to drunkenness with his subjects, unknowing that this was a sin. Taking on the figure of a Brahman, with a jar of moderate size hanging down from his left side, he showed himself, standing in the air, to the king, crying out, "Who wants to buy this jar?" "Who are you?" the king asked. "Later you will know but now be intent on purchasing this jar if you are willing to take the consequences," answered Sakra. On the king's asking what sort of jar it was, Sakra declared that it held that from which direst results would come, and then he described drunkenness accurately. The sermon so impressed the king that he resolved to give up drinking and wanted to reward the preacher. Sakra showed himself in his own real shape and disappeared. The king and his subjects gave up drinking.[18] (Top of banner, right and left.)

» 45 «

Tanka 9

Eighteenth birth succession, of rich royal family (*rgyal-rigs phyug-pai skyes-pai rabs-te bcu-brgyad-pa*)

The Bodhisattva was born in a wealthy family, noted for virtue and "like a refreshing well" in sharing its store of goods. Brought up with accomplished education and knowledge of the world, he had nevertheless familiarized himself with world-renunciation. On the death of his parents, he distributed all his wealth and became a hermit, with an abode far distant on a woody plateau in the vicinity of a town. A friend of his father's, having heard of his retreat, visited him there and tried to persuade him to return to the paternal house, praising the condition of a family man. In answer, the young man delivered a long speech, so impressing his visitor with the advantage of hermit life, that the visitor showed "high respect to the Great Being by entertaining him with a meal in the most distinguished manner."[19] (Lowest quarter of banner, right and left.)

Nineteenth birth succession, is about lotus stalks (*padmai rtsa-bai sykes-pai rabs-te bcu-dgu-pa-o*)

The Bodhisattva was born in an illustrious family of Brahmans, far-famed for virtue and for freedom from vice. He had six younger brothers and a sister, endowed as was he. When his parents died, he declared to his brothers and sister that he would leave the home to them and take up the homeless life. They declared that they would go with him, and thus they gave away all they had. With a comrade and a male and a female servant, who insisted on accompanying them, they retired into the forest. Here they built as many huts of leaves as they numbered, at a distance from one another, hidden in the shadow of the leaves. On each fifth day they assembled to hear the Bodhisattva preach the Law.

The maid still attended upon them by drawing eatable lotus stalks out of the lake, putting equal shares upon large lotus leaves on the shore, and announcing the mealtime by striking one piece of wood on another.

Sakra, having heard of their irreproachable way of living, came to try them by stealing away the Bodhisattva's share before the others came to get their portions. The Bodhisattva, thinking that one of the others had probably taken his food, returned quietly to his hut, saying nothing to anyone.

The five days passed. When they all assembled to hear the Law, they saw the leanness of his body, the hollow of his cheeks, the sunkenness of his eyes, and they asked him whence came this state. He told them. None could understand this, for Sakra had obstructed their power of penetration. One after another, each took an oath that he had not done this evil deed. Each one made a wish that he who took the lotus stalks might have poured down on him all worldly enjoyments—the worst curse, of course, that could be pronounced on hermits. A yaksha, an elephant, and a monkey who had been coming to that forest to hear the Law took the same oath.

Then Sakra, aroused to astonishment, appeared in his own brilliant shape and asked them why they had so spoken. The Bodhisattva explained to him the injuriousness of worldly enjoyments, whereupon Sakra confessed that it was he who had taken the lotus stalks. He handed them over, asked pardon, and disappeared on the spot.[20] (The scenes begin in the second quarter from the bottom of the banner, to the right, and move across to the left and up center left.)

Twentieth birth succession, is as a treasurer (*tshong-dpon skyes-pai rabs nyu-pa-o*)

The Bodhisattva was born a king's treasurer, illustrious for his learning, his noble family, his modest behavior. He made his wealth flow in all directions in charity. Once when he had gone on business to the king's palace, his mother-in-law came to visit her daughter and inquired how her husband was treating her. The daughter answered that it would be difficult for even a hermit to be as virtuous as her husband. The mother, being a little deaf and catching the word hermit, thought that her son-in-law had become one. Bursting into tears, she commiserated and vociferated, so that people gathered. The daughter, confused, thought that her mother had come to report to her that her husband had become a hermit! She swooned.

The treasurer, returning home, saw the crowd. He heard complaints and much lamenting about his having become a hermit. Considering it a high honor to be thought of as renouncing the world, he returned to the king and asked his permission to become a homeless one. The king tried to dissuade him, but he was inflexible, arguing that a high opinion must be acted up to. The king gave permission. And the Great Being, in spite of protestations of his whole entourage of kinsmen and friends, went away to his hut of leaves.[21] (The family scene, as the treasurer returns home, begins in the third quarter from bottom, to the right; at the left, top, the treasurer returns to the king to ask permission; at the right, top, the treasurer is in his hermit hut.)

Tanka 10

Twenty-first birth succession, having to do with crown-of-head perfection of-fering (*gtsug-phud byang-chub-kyi skyes-pai rabs-te nyir-gcig*)

The Bodhisattva was born in a noble family of Brahmans, wealthy, virtuous. As he grew up, becoming familiarized with world-renunciation through merit in former existences, he longed for the Self, and so he parted with his fair hair and beard, in token of becoming an ascetic. His wife also cut off her hair, and she donned the orange-colored robes along with him, insisting on accompanying him in spite of his efforts to dissuade her because of the roughness of such a life.

They lived in the forest. There, on a day after the Great Being had arisen from profound meditation and was sewing rags together to make clothes, while his wife sat near by in the shade of a tree, meditating as he had taught her, the king of that country came on a tour through the groves to view their springtime splendor. On seeing the Bodhisattva, the king drew near, greeting him respectfully. But then he observed the female hermit's beauty, and he commanded his retinue to carry her off to his zenana, although knowing that she must be the ascetic's companion. The hermit remained in a state of quiet; he explained to the king, who could not understand this way of acting, how he kept anger from arising. Thereupon the king gave the hermit's wife back, and himself became the Great Being's attendant.[22] (Across the bottom of the banner, from right to left.)

Twenty-second birth succession, is as a goose (*ngang-par skyes-pai rabs-te nyer-gnyis-pa-o*)

This story[23] is told in Chapter I, pages 22-23.

Twenty-third birth succession, as One-Having-Highest-Perfection-and-Holiness (*byang-chub chen-por skyes-pai rabs-te gnyer-gsum-pa*)

The Bodhisattva was born as a householder. Having studied worldly branches of learning thoroughly, he became a wandering ascetic, named Mahābodhi. Going on exerting himself for the benefit of the world by mastering the science of the Law, he became so skillful in conversing with people that wherever he went he was cherished by the learned. Wandering about with the object of doing good to men, he came to the realm of a king who had heard of him and had already had a place built for him in his own pleasure gardens, in anticipation of his coming. The king received him with honor, and constantly conversed with him on the Law, which caused the king's ministers to envy him and to inspire the king with suspicion against him as probably being the spy of some enemy.

Lending ear to these suggestions, the king began to treat the ascetic coldly. The ascetic did not mind this until he saw the lack of respect of the courtiers, and so he made ready for departure. The king, troubled, sought to persuade him to remain. While they spoke together, the king's favorite dog, who had been friendly to the ascetic as long as his master had been, barked at him in a hostile manner. The Great Being called the king's attention to this as the best evidence of the changed feelings of the king himself. The king then yielded to the ascetic's strong determination to go but begged him to return soon. The Bodhisattva did not make a positive promise, but expressed the wish "to see you another time, when there may be some indispensable reason for coming." With these words he departed.

He took up his abode in a forest and went into deep meditation, in which he attained the four contemplations and the five kinds of transcendent knowledge. Then he remembered the king, with great compassion, and saw in his mind that the king was in the hands of the five ministers, each of whom had a false doctrine with which he tempted the king so as to show that for him there was no lawlessness. Resolving to save the king, the ascetic created a large monkey by magic, and clothed himself in the monkey's hide, causing the body to disappear. Thus he came before the king.

After the salutations, the king asked, "By whom was that monkey skin given to you?" "I myself killed the monkey and took his skin." The ministers exclaimed malignantly at this awful sin—the murder of a living being. The Bodhisattva, on his part, showed to each one of them that from the standpoint of each one's particular doctrine there was no sin in it. Then he explained that he had not killed any monkey but had only performed a magic trick. Thus he led both king and ministers away from false doctrine to the Excellent Path. Directly he mounted into

the sky, worshiped by the assembly, and went again to his forest place.[24]
(The scenes begin at the top of the banner, to the left, where Mahābodhi is seen with the king and his ministers; right, center, he shows
the king how the dog behaves; right, top, he meditates in the forest;
center, right, he comes back in the monkey skin; top, he flies away to
his forest place.)

Twenty-fourth birth succession, as a Great Ape. [The tanka presumably portraying the 24th, 25th, and 26th birth successions is missing. This would
be Tanka 10 if the series were complete to the number of 15, as indicated
by the inscription on Tanka 13 in the St. Louis series.]

In a blessed region on one side of the Himavat (the Himalaya Mountains), clothed in magnificent forests, watered by many mountain
streams, abounding in deep chasms and precipices, resounding with the
humming of bees and with winds stirring the many kinds of trees bearing flowers and fruits, the Bodhisattva came to life as a great ape of
immense size, living alone. Even in such a state, he still had consciousness of the Dharma, being grateful, noble-natured, patient. His compassion, as if retained by attachment, never left him. Like an ascetic, he
lived on the leaves and fruits of forest trees, and he helped such creatures
as he met within the bounds of his ability.

One such creature was a certain man who, in search of a strayed cow,
lost his way and roamed about until he reached that place. Exhausted,
he sat down at the foot of a tree. Looking about, he saw on the ground
some tawny tinduka fruits (eatable fruit but sour; food for the poor),
fallen down from ripeness. Enjoying them in appeasing his great hunger
and wishing to find out whence they had come, he discovered a tree
with its roots on the edge of a sloping bank of a waterfall. Its downhang-
ing branches were loaded with the very ripe fruit, tawny at the ends.
Craving more of the fruit, he went up the slope, climbed the tree to
a loaded branch overhanging the precipice, and went along it to get

the fruit. Suddenly the branch broke off. He fell with it, on to a precipice surrounded on all sides by steep rock walls, and was thrown into deep water. Protected by the leaves, he came out unhurt. He looked on all sides for a way out but saw none. Overwhelmed by despair, he lamented at great length. Amidst swarms of mosquitoes and in darkness, he lived on water and the tinduka fruits for some days.

Now that great ape, wandering about looking for food, came there, almost as if the branches of the tinduka tree, waving in the wind, had beckoned him. Climbing the tree, he looked over the waterfall and saw the wretched man lying there, pale, hungry, emaciated. He fixed his eyes compellingly on the man and called down in a human voice: "You are in this abyss inaccessible to men. Who are you? How came you to be here?" The man cast his eyes upward toward the great ape, bowed his head, folded his hands as a suppliant, and said: "I am a man, Illustrious Being." Then he described how he came to be there and besought the great ape as "protector of troops of monkeys" to be "also my protector." Stirred with boundless pity, the Great Being comforted him with kind words and threw down tinduka and other fruits to him. Then, with the thought of rescue, he went to another place and exercised himself in climbing with a stone the weight of a man on his back. When satisfied that he would be able to get the man out, he descended to him and told him to climb on his back and hold fast, "while I bring out both thee and the usefulness of my body." With reverential bowing to the ape, the man mounted the great back. After extreme difficulty the ape succeeded in getting him out. Then, exhausted, he lay down upon a stone slab to rest, not suspecting danger from one whose benefactor he had been. He asked the man to keep watch in this place easily accessible to animals so that no one would kill him while he rested. With honest mien, the man promised.

However, after the Great Being had fallen asleep, the man conceived wicked thoughts in asking himself how he was to become strong enough to escape from this wild place, where the garnering of roots cost hard effort, and fruits were got only by chance. In the body of the ape he would have sufficient food to keep him going long enough to escape. But the ape must be killed while asleep, for there would be no possibility of killing him in an open fight. Therefore he at once lifted a stone and made it fall down on the head of the great ape. But his hand trembled so from weakness and haste that the stone, instead of striking with its whole weight, only bruised the ape's head with one of its edges, falling to the ground with a great noise, which awakened the ape.

The Bodhisattva jumped up hastily and looked about to see who had attacked him. He beheld only the man whom he had rescued, now in an attitude of shame, ashy-pale, timid, downcast, his body covered with drops of sweat, afraid to raise his eyes to his benefactor. The Great Being, realizing then that this man was the evildoer, was moved with compassion for him who, not thinking of his own happiness, had committed such a vile deed. Eyes wet with tears, and unmindful of the pain of his bruises, he lamented that he had saved the man from one precipice only to have him fall down another. And he declared that his bruises grieved him less than the suffering in his mind over the fact that it was on his own account that the man had plunged into evil and that he did not have the power of wiping off that sin.

"Well, then, go with me, keeping by my side, for thou art much to be distrusted," the Great Being adjured him. "I will conduct thee out of this forest, the abode of manifold dangers, again into the path which leads to the dwellings of men."

Thus the Great Being conducted him to the border of the inhabited region. There he pointed out the further way, bade him a happy journey, and wished him avoidance of evil acts, since the harvest of their consequence is extremely painful. Having instructed him as if he were his disciple, the High-Minded One turned back again to his abode in the forest.

But the man, tormented now by "the blazing fire of remorse," was struck with leprosy. His figure became changed. His skin erupted with vesicles, which turned to ulcers that burst, covering his body with putrid matter. Wherever he went, he was an object of horror. Thinking him to be an embodied Devil, people drove him away with clods or clubs and cursed him. One day, while roaming through a forest, he was seen by the king, who was hunting there. On observing this horrible creature, so little clad with remains of dirty garments as hardly to cover his shame, the king, fearful yet curious, asked him what he was—a *Preta*, or a goblin, or a *Pūtana* ("a horrible-looking ghost living in cemeteries and feeding on human flesh").

"I am a man, Great King, not a spirit," the man answered, going on, when pressed, to relate what he had done. He said that he deemed his present state "only the blossom of the tree sown by that treacherous deed against my friend. Oh, surely, its fruits will be more miserable than this." What he had learned out of his suffering, he developed into advice to the king: "Thus, knowing power and the consequences of good and evil behavior with respect to friends, O king, hold fast to the road followed by the virtuous."[25]

Twenty-fifth birth succession, as a Śarabha. [This seems to refer to a fabulous deer, eight-legged, in strength a match for elephants and lions.]

The Bodhisattva, it is said, once lived far from men in the remote part of a certain forest that had many trees, roots, and shrubs embedded in thick, high grass untrodden by travelers. But the many animals whose dwelling place it was had cut it into channels, and it was full of anthills and holes. He was solidly built, vigorous, swift. His beautifully colored body was in the shape of a forest animal, but he possessed the intellectual faculties of a man, was friendly toward other animals, and lived like an ascetic on grasses, leaves, and water, longing for detachment, showing compassion to all living beings.

Tanka 10

Patience in the face of insult
Pain-bearing for others
Maintaining bodhi holiness

PLATE X   COURTESY CITY ART MUSEUM OF ST. LOUIS

PLATE XI

COURTESY CITY ART MUSEUM OF ST. LOUIS

Tanka 11

Saving the monkey troop
Manifesting forbearance
Descent from Brahmaloka

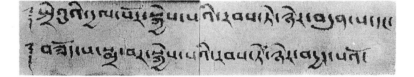

It happened that the king who ruled that country came near this part of the forest mounted on his excellent horse and holding bent bow and arrow in pursuit of deer. Carried away by his swift horse, far from his retinue of elephants, horses, chariots, men, he saw at a distance the Great Being. Resolved on killing him, keeping his bow ready, he spurred his horse toward the High-Minded One, who, to avoid an act of violence and anger, took to flight with utmost swiftness. Meeting a large hole, the Bodhisattva jumped quickly over it, as if it were but a small puddle, and continued his flight. But when the king's horse arrived at that hole, it hesitated, standing still, so that the king, with bow in hands, lost his balance, tumbled down from his horse, and fell headlong into the large hole.

Not hearing the sound of hoofs any longer, and wondering if the king had turned back, the Bodhisattva turned about, looked around, and saw the horse standing at the edge of the hole. He reasoned that the king must surely have fallen into that chasm, where there was no shade tree or water. Certainly, he would not have dismounted to rest or hunt alone, leaving the horse there, nor was there any jungle in which he could hide. Convinced of the fate of the king, he felt great commiseration for him who was one moment surrounded by splendor, and the next moment, perhaps with broken bones, in this hole. Impelled by compassion, he went to the brink of the chasm and saw the king struggling there, his armor covered with dust, his diadem and garments in disarray, afflicted obviously by pains from his fall. With tears welling up in his eyes, the Great Being addressed the king modestly and kindly, comforting him. He explained that he was a forest animal, that he could be trusted, and that he would rescue the king if commanded to do so.

Astounded at such an attitude of pity from one whose enemy he himself was, the king felt shame arise in him. "It is I who am the animal, the brute," he thought; "he is some Being with only the shape of a Śarabha." Accepting, then, the Great Being's offer, he answered that his pain from the fall did not torment him so much as his offense against such a pure being as this deer. The Bodhisattva, taking this as acceptance of his offer of rescue, exercised himself with a stone the weight of a man on his back. When confident that he could bear such a weight, he went down into the hole, asked the king to mount on his back, and climbed upward with astonishing swiftness, "holding high the forepart of his body, resembling some (stone) elephant rising in the air as is represented on arches." Rejoicing, he accompanied the king to his horse and showed him the way to the capital. Then he turned to go back into the forest. But the king, moved with gratitude, embraced him, saying, "This life of mine is at thy disposal, O Śarabha!," and invited him to go home with him. The Bodhisattva, however, while eulogizing the king's behavior, declared that this could not be, since the pleasure of men is of one sort, that of forest animals another. But if the king really wished to do something for him, he should "desist from hunting, for animals, being of dull intellect but subject to the same feelings as men, are worth pitying." Weaving this into a little sermon on virtuous action, he firmly grounded the king in matters related to the future life, after which he entered his forest abode followed with respectful looks from the king.[26]

Twenty-sixth birth succession, as a ruru deer. [The tanka for this birth succession is lacking in the St. Louis series. For a portrayal of the scenes, see Tanka A in Chapter V.]

At one time, it is said, the Bodhisattva lived as a ruru deer in a remote part of a great wilderness overgrown with rich vegetation and inhabited by many kinds of deer and by yaks, elephants, oxen, buffaloes, antelopes, boars, panthers, hyenas, tigers, wolves, lions, bears. Among them the ruru deer—conspicuous by its brilliant golden hue and large mild blue eyes, the soft hair of its body adorned with spots of color as of rubies, sapphires, emeralds, and beryls, its shining horns and hoofs

—moved like a "treasury of jewels." Knowing that his body was a very desirable object, and aware of the pitiless nature of men, he frequented tracks not used by them. His keen intellect enabled him to avoid the traps and snares of huntsmen, and he warned the animals that followed him, as a teacher or father.

In that wilderness he once heard distressful cries for help from some man being carried away by a nearby stream swollen by rains. He rushed out of the thicket, calling out comforting words he had been accustomed to use in hundreds of previous existences to help afflicted ones. "Do not fear! Do not fear!" He brought out these words in a plain human voice, over and over, loudly, until, emerging from the forest, he saw the man, like a precious present being brought to him by the stream. He entered its rapidly running current, placed himself across the man's way, and told him to cling fast to him. The man, in a paroxysm of fear, climbed on his back.

In spite of the weight on his back and the violence of the water, the Bodhisattva, his vigor intact because of the "excellence of his nature," forced his way to the bank. There, relieving the man's fatigue and pain, and obtaining in himself rejoicing, he warmed the man's cold limbs with his own body and then pointed out the way home. The man, however, declaring that no friend or kinsman of his was capable of doing for him what the deer had done, said, "This life of mine is yours," and if that life could be spent for some matter to the deer's interest, he would consider himself highly favored. "Gratitude," the deer replied, "is a virtue." Let the man, then, not be induced to relate to anyone how he had been rescued, since his rescuer's beautiful figure made him too desirable a prey, and the hearts of men, covetous, possess little mercy. "So, then, you will please me by doing what I said." The man promised, made a salutation, circumambulated the deer, and set out for home. (The scenes begin in the lower right corner of Tanka A, which shows the man coming down current toward the spot where the deer is resting, then getting on the back of the deer, who has entered the stream; the deer getting him to shore and warming him; the man making his promise to the deer; the man back in his home place with the king.)

At that time, there lived in that country a queen who saw true dreams. No matter how extraordinary were the dreams she had, they became true. While asleep one night, she had a dream, about daybreak, in which she saw a ruru deer, shining like a heap of jewels, standing on a throne, surrounded by the king and his retinue, and preaching the Law in a human, articulate, distinct voice. In astonishment over her dream, she woke up at the beating of drums—a ritual performed every morning to arouse the king from sleep.

At the first chance she went to see the king. He received her with honor and affection. She related her dream and begged him to try to obtain that jewel-deer to make his zenana resplendent. (In the lower part of Tanka A, center, the queen relates her dream to the king.) Having experience of the truth of her dreams, the king readily ordered all his huntsmen to search for that deer and had proclamation made in his capital, day after day, that there existed a gold-skinned deer spotted with shining jewel-like colors. "It is celebrated in the holy texts, and some have sighted it. Whoever will show that deer, to him the king gives a very rich village and full ten lovely women."

Again and again, the man who had been rescued heard that proclamation, torn between doing something to relieve his suffering from poverty and the gratitude he still had in him from the great benefit he had received. Finally he argued himself out of his gratitude and went to the king (on Tanka A, to the left of the king and queen seated together) and told him he knew that excellent deer and his abode. "Tell me to whom I shall show him."

"Well, friend, show him to me," said the king. He put on his hunting dress, left the capital with a large body of army, and let himself be conducted by the man to the riverside. Encircling the adjoining forest with his whole force, he himself, bearing his bow, with a select number of resolute faithful men, entered the thicket, still led by the man. Discovering the deer, then, who was unsuspectingly staying in his spot in the forest, the man exclaimed to the king: "Here, here is that precious deer, Your Majesty! May Your Majesty deign to look at him and be careful." Saying this, eager to point out the deer, he raised his arm, only to have his hand fall off his arm as if a sword had cut it off!

The king, wanting to get sight of the deer, let his eyes follow in the direction pointed out by the man, and in the midst of that dark wood he saw a body shining like a treasury of jewels, like "the fire of lightning out of the womb of the cloud." Desirous of catching the deer, the king curved his bow, adjusted his arrow, and went up toward him that he might hit him. The Bodhisattva, however, having heard the noise of people on every side, had concluded that he was surrounded; and so, with the king advancing to shoot him, and knowing that he could not run away, he addressed the king in distinct, articulate language: "Stop a moment, mighty prince. Do not hit me. Pray, satisfy my curiosity first, and tell me who may have discovered my abode to you, far as it is from the paths of men."

Touched by such wonderful speech in human voice, the king showed him the man with the point of his arrow, saying, "This man." But the Bodhisattva, knowing the man, called shame upon him, with "Better is it to take a log out of water than to save an ungrateful person from it." Thus he reproached him who had repaid exertion on his behalf in this manner. Could the man not see that he was destroying his own happiness at the same time?

Perplexed, the king asked why he was speaking with such censure. "I spoke sharp words in order to prevent this man from attempting to do such a thing again," the Bodhisattva explained. Then he described the rescue experience.

On being questioned, the man, in great shame, confessed his ingratitude. The king reviled him and bent his bow to kill him. But the Bodhisattva, deeply gripped by commiseration, placed himself between them. "Stop, Your Majesty! Do not strike one already stricken!" (The left lower corner quarter of Tanka A shows the encircled thicket, the man's hand falling off, the king aiming at the man after discovering his ingratitude, and the deer stopping him.) Going on to show how really deeply the man was stricken both in this world and in the next, the Bodhisattva counseled that the king, rather, should pity the man. "And if he wanted to obtain something by so acting, let not his rash deed lack that reward. For lo, I am standing here with bent head awaiting thy orders." Overcome by such magnanimity, the king exclaimed, "Well said! Well said, Holy Being!" He promised to bestow the wealth the man had coveted, and to the Bodhisattva deer he gave permission to go freely in the kingdom wherever it pleased him.

Accepting this royal boon, the ruru deer asked to be given orders, "that our meeting here may afford thee profit and that I may be of some use to you." Thereupon the king made the deer mount his royal chariot, worshiped him as his teacher, and led him with great pomp to the capital. Giving him a reception due a guest, he invited him to place himself on the royal throne (left side of Tanka A, near center), before which the king, with his wife and the whole retinue of officers assembled, besought him to preach the Law, because "There is a great diversity of opinions among men concerning the Law, but thou possessest the certainty of the Law."

Then the Bodhisattva raised his voice, and, in words spoken distinctly in a soft tone and elegantly composed, he preached to the royal assembly the Law, the summary of which he believed to be "Mercy to the creatures." There followed a matchless little sermon on Mercy, in which, the wise firmly declare, "the whole of righteousness is contained." The king, praising these words of the ruru deer, became, as did also his townsmen and landsmen, intent on acting up to the Law of Righteousness. And he granted security to all quadrupeds and birds.[27] (Translated in full from the Kanjur, in Chapter V.)

Tanka 11

Twenty-seventh birth succession, as king of monkeys and . . . (*spreui rgyal-por skyes-pai rabs-te nyer-bdun-pa dang . . .*)

The Bodhisattva was born in a blessed region in the heart of the Himalayas. He became the chief of a troop of monkeys who lived on a large banyan tree, subsisting on its fruits. One branch of the tree stretched out over a river, and the chief expressly cautioned his troop to cull the fruits from that branch before they could mature and fall, or they would not be able to eat fruit from the other branches. However, they overlooked one fruit which, grown ripe, fell into the river and was borne down where the king came to bathe. So pleased was he with it, that he decided to find out where it came from. With his army he marched up the river until he saw the tree and on it the monkeys, which he ordered to be killed, since they were eating the wonderful fruit.

The Bodhisattva, encouraging the frightened monkeys, climbed to the top of the tree and jumped from there to a mountain peak. He knew the other monkeys could not jump that far, so he found on the mountain slope a strong liana, bound it to his feet, and jumped back, catching hold of a branch of the tree so as to form a bridge, across which, at his signal, the troop made haste to pass. Astounded, the king ordered his army, which stood in amazement, cautiously to take the leader. This they did.

They put him on a soft couch, because he had lost consciousness from exhaustion. When he had recovered his senses, the king asked him why he had acted thus. Answering that it was his duty as king of the monkeys, he pronounced a sermon on the duties of a king. Then, leaving his "body paralyzed in its functions by the excess of his pains, he mounted to heaven."[28] (Across the bottom of the banner, from right to left.)

The king-of-monkeys story is also portrayed on Tanka A. (The progression of scenes begins left center, above the deer on the throne, with the bringing of mangoes to the king; weaves across the top to the right, with monkeys escaping over the bridge made for them by their leader, who, exhausted, has fallen into the net held by two of the king's men; at the top right corner the Bodhisattva monkey leader, resuscitated, preaches the Law to the king.)

Twenty-eighth birth succession, is as Kshāntivādin, One-Preaching-Forbearance
(*bzod-pa smra-bar skyes-pai rabs-te nyer-brgyad-pa-o*)

"Truly to those who have imbibed the virtue of forbearance and are great in keeping their tranquillity there is nothing unbearable."

The Bodhisattva was born as one who became an ascetic forsaking the world. He settled in a forest place that was like a lovely garden and was visited there by "such people as were lovers of virtue and desirous of salvation." So constantly did he preach on the power of forbearance that he was named Kshāntivādin (patience- or forbearance-preacher). One summer day the king of the country came into that forest on pleasure, with his retinue of women. After much enjoyment, he fell asleep.

His women wandered about, wantonly stripping the place of flowers, and came to the hermitage, where the High-Minded One sat under a tree "like the embodied Dharma." Subdued by his pure and gracious presence, they sat down humbly before him while he preached the Law "in such terms as were easily understood by women." Meanwhile, the king awoke and asked where his royal wives were. Being informed that they were wandering in the forest, he traced them, with his eunuchs following, to the hermitage. There, seized with fury at seeing them sit listening to the ascetic, he poured invectives on the holy man. The queens, interceding ineffectually for the holy man, were led away by the eunuchs, who knew their master's terrible wrath.

The infuriated king drew his sword and began to hack the hermit to pieces. He hewed off hands, feet, ears, and nose, but the forbearance-preacher kept quiet. On contemplating his work, the king felt a great heat, and as he came out of the forest the earth opened up with a crash, fire leaped out, and he was swallowed down into hell. Alarmed by the fearful noise, the people assembled in fright, and the king's ministers begged the hermit not to destroy the whole country as he had destroyed the king. Appeasing and instructing them, "that foremost of the Munis left his earthly residence and ascended to heaven."[29] (The scenes begin below the center of the banner, toward the right, with the king coming into the pleasure forest on his horse; at right center, the king is sleeping, the women are leaving; at left center, the women are listening to the hermit; at left top, the king is hacking the hermit to pieces, and then is drawn down into hell.)

The story of Kshāntivādin is also portrayed on Tanka A. (The progression of scenes begins below the end of the monkey story and descends down the right side: the Bodhisattva as ascetic in his retreat; the king sleeping on a couch in the grove; the queens grouped about the ascetic listening to his teaching; the king, with drawn sword, about to hack the ascetic to pieces; the ascetic sitting in quietness with hands and feet cut off; the king being drawn down into the hell which had opened to engulf him; the prime ministers begging the Bodhisattva to be propitious to their country.)

Twenty-ninth birth succession, (in the world) of Brahma (*tshangs-pai skyes-pai rabs 29*)

The Bodhisattva was born in Brahmaloka (the third region of happiness, above the Deva world, of which Sakra is Lord). Because he still longed to benefit others, he at one time passed his eyes over the Region of Sensuality below, to find a proper sphere of action for his compassion. There he saw Aṅgadinna, King of Videha, who, cherishing heretical opinions, denied the existence of another world and the building up of a future destiny out of good or evil actions.

Descending from heaven, the Bodhisattva appeared before the king, who asked, "Who are you?" "One of those Devarshis of Brahma's world," the High-Minded One answered and proceeded to speak of that other world. Listening, but not convinced, the king interrupted with an ironical remark that if indeed there was another world, let the Devarshi give him 500 cash and he would give him back 1,000 in the other world. Because of such obstinate disbelief, the Bodhisattva pointed out the tortures of hell. Frightened at this, the king turned to the true path; and the High-Minded One disappeared. (At the top right of the banner, the Bodhisattva is in discussion with the king; at the top center, the Bodhisattva is in the air above Sakra.)

Tanka 12

Thirtieth birth succession, as an elephant and . . . (*glang-po-cher skyes-pai rabs-te sum-bcu-pa dang* . . .)

The Bodhisattva was born as a great elephant. He lived in solitude in a forest remote from the habitations of men. While wandering near the border of that forest one day, he heard a great clamor as of many people crying for help. He went in that direction and met 700 people —the remnant of 1,000 who had been exiled by their king. The Great Being conceived the idea of feeding them with his own flesh. He therefore directed them to a large lake below the mountain, near which they were to find the body of an elephant for food. Its intestines would serve for bags in which to carry water for the rest of their journey.

Having induced them to set out, he himself ran quickly by another way to the top of the mountain. While standing there, "he strengthened his determination, truly, by representing to his mind something like this: 'This performance does not tend to the attainment of a high state for myself, neither the magnificence of a king of men, the possessor of the royal umbrella, nor Heaven (Deva world) with the singular flavor of its surpassing enjoyments, nor the bliss of Brahma's world, nor even the happiness of release (*nirvāṇa*); but if there be any merit of mine in thus striving to help those men lost in the wilderness, may I become by it the Savior of the World, of those creatures erring in the wilderness of Sangsāra!' " Thus, not minding the painful death he must suffer, he threw himself down, with celestial happenings attending his self-sacrifice. The wanderers found his body, recognized it as their Savior, and obeyed his counsel to use the body for food, the intestines for waterskins. They safely crossed the wilderness.[30] (Across the bottom of the banner.)

Thirty-first birth succession, having to do with the son of Sudāsa (*su-da-sai bui skyes-pai rabs-te so-gcig-pa*). [Below this inscription is written *bcu-bzhi-pa*, which means "fourteenth." This, together with the inscription on our Tanka 13, indicates that there were 15 banners in the set.]

The Bodhisattva happened to be born in the illustrious royal family of Kuru. He was named Sutasoma. Because of his virtues and learning he was raised to the rank of heir apparent. As a great lover of well-turned religious sentences, he paid the most distinguished reward to those who attended him with such fare. And so he was visited, while staying in a pleasure park, by a certain Brahman professing the art of making beautiful verses. But before the Brahman could present his accomplishment, a great noise arose, and frightened servants ran up shouting that the son of Sudāsa had come. The Bodhisattva asked, although he already knew, who that person was. He listened while they explained that once a king named Sudāsa went hunting and was carried by his horse into the depths of the forest, where he met a lioness with whom he had relations and who bore him a child, male and human, whom Sudāsa brought up and left as his successor when he himself "passed away to the city of the Celestials."

From his mother the boy inherited a taste for different sorts of raw flesh, including human flesh. When he became king, he killed some of his subjects so that he might have human flesh to eat. His subjects at last resolved to kill him. Becoming afraid, the son of Sudāsa promised the spirits (*bhūtas*) a sacrifice of 100 princes if they would deliver him from danger. For this purpose, he had already carried away many royal princes; and now, the servants said, he had come for Sutasoma.

The Bodhisattva, who knew all this, felt compassion for the son of Sudāsa and set his mind on a design to cure him. So he ordered the guard of his harem to attend to their ordinary duties; and he ordered his female lifeguard not to block the man-eater's way. Then the Bodhisattva called out, while the man-eater was in the act of pursuing the royal army, "Halloo! Here am I, Sutasoma. Turn to me!"

Said the son of Sudāsa, "You are the very man I am pursuing," and ran to him, placed him on his shoulder, and carried him up to his seat—"a place encumbered with the corpses of slain men, and wet with blood horribly moistening the ground"—where he set him down, staring at him because of his exceeding beauty.

Now the Bodhisattva remembered the poor Brahman who had come to him to get a present for his verses. Thinking of that versemaker's great disappointment, he shed tears. The son of Sudāsa, believing the prince to be afraid, scoffed at him. Sutasoma explained why he was weeping and begged the son of Sudāsa to allow him to go home, hear the Brahman's verses, and then return. The man-eater had no faith in his promise to return. Sutasoma reminded him that he had come willingly, had perhaps even wished to come, and so would certainly return after fulfilling his debt to the Brahman. To try Sutasoma, the man-eater let him go, saying that meanwhile he would dress the funeral pile for him. Returning home, Sutasoma sent for the Brahman, learned from

Tanka 12

Preserving 700 lives
Converting a man-eater

PLATE XII

COURTESY CITY ART MUSEUM OF ST. LOUIS

PLATE XIII

COURTESY CITY ART MUSEUM OF ST. LOUIS

Tanka 13

Being brought up in an iron hous
Behaving wisely toward torment
Enduring ungratefulness

him a tetrad of verses, and generously rewarded him. Then, in spite of the remonstrances of his father, he returned to the son of Sudāsa, who was overwhelmed with astonishment.

Sutasoma said that now that he had heard the Brahman's four verses —and inasmuch as he did not recollect ever having taken any step toward evil—he was ready for death. "So, dress me for your sacrifice and eat me." On hearing this language, the son of Sudāsa was moved to tears of tenderness, and the darkness of his wicked nature vanished. He begged to hear the Brahman's verses, and constructed for Sutasoma a teacher's seat, from which the verses were pronounced. So pleased with them was the son of Sudāsa that he offered Sutasoma anything he wanted, even his own life. "Well, then," Sutasoma replied, "take the vow of veracity; give up injuring living beings; release all your prisoners, nobody excepted; and nevermore eat human flesh, O you hero among men!" The son of Sudāsa consented to the first three but asked the fourth to be changed, since it would be impossible for him to abstain from human flesh. "What are the first three worth without the last?" asked Sutasoma, and he continued to preach until at last the son of Sudāsa surrendered. The imprisoned princes were set free, and all returned with Sutasoma and the son of Sudāsa to their respective countries.[31] (At the left of the banner, below center, Sutasoma is by the lotus pond, the Brahman before him; above center, at the left, he is seized by the son of Sudāsa; at right center, he feeds the Brahman, listens to him; at top right, he returns to the son of Sudāsa.)

Tanka 13

Thirty-second birth succession, as Ayogriha, One-Brought-Up-in-an-Iron-House
(*lcags-kyi khyim-na skyes-pai rabs-te so-gnyis-pa*)

The Bodhisattva was born in a "certain royal family distinguished for modest behavior and surpassing luster" and of "prosperity and riches without hindrance." Now, since every prince born to the king so far had died, and since the deaths were attributed to the power of evil spirits called yakshas, the king had a house of iron built, embellished with magnificent figures of gold and silver and jewels, as the lying-in place for the birth of his next son. There the son was brought up, instructed by illustrious teachers in many branches of science and in the knowledge of sacred texts. Because of his loveliness and the brilliancy of his virtues, the youth was loved by all.

On the occasion of the Kaumudi festival, he was permitted by his royal father to mount the royal chariot for a drive through the capital. All along the way he was received by crowds of townsmen, who praised him and worshiped him with bent heads and folded hands. Contemplating this spectacle, he regained remembrance of his former birth. Meditating on the transitoriness of everything earthly, he returned to his father only to beg him, with folded hands, to let him leave for the penance-forest. Sore with grief, the father begged him to say why he wished to do such a thing when everyone loved him so much. But the Bodhisattva, in a long discourse, convinced his father that such was the highest outcome for him in life. Renouncing, then, his royal bliss, the prince took up his abode in the penance-forest. There he acquired "dhyanas [meditations] of immense extent" and established mankind in them. Then he mounted to Brahma's world.[32] (Lower half of banner.)

Thirty-third birth succession, as chief of wild buffaloes (*ma-he-rgod-kyi khyu-mchog-la skyes-pai rabs so-gsum-pa*)

The Bodhisattva at one time lived in a forest region as "a wild buffalo bull of grim appearance, owing to his being dirty with mud, and so dark of complexion that he resembled a moving piece of a dark-blue cloud." He was in animal state; yet "in consequence of his keen understanding, he was exerting himself to practice righteousness." Now, there lived also in that forest a wicked monkey, who took great delight in tormenting and torturing the Great Being, who bore all with patience. A yaksha, being there at the time when the monkey was riding on the buffalo, placed himself in the way, telling the Bodhisattva he should not let the monkey so do. The Great Being replied with a sermon on forbearance, by which he hoped, he said, to awake the conscience of the monkey. The yaksha eulogized him, threw the monkey off his back, and taught the buffalo a preservative charm, then disappeared on the spot.[33] (Top left of banner.)

Thirty-fourth birth succession, as a (female) woodpecker (*bya-shing-rta [rgon]-moi skyes-pai rabs-te so-bzhi-pa rdzogs-so bco-lnga-pa*). [The expression *rdzogs-so* means "It is finished"; and *bco-lnga-pa* means "fifteenth." This shows that Tanka 13 in the St. Louis series is actually the last tanka in a series of fifteen, and that two tankas are lacking in the series.]

The Bodhisattva lived in a forest place as a woodpecker, distinguished by beautiful feathers of manifold colors. Though in the state of a bird, he did not follow that way of living. He abstained from harming living beings, ate fruits and seeds of trees, preached precepts to others, and helped those in distress. (Although both the inscription and the text of the Kanjur version refer to a "female" woodpecker, "he" is used all the way through, perhaps to keep the reference to the Bodhisattva.)

Once when he was rambling through the forest, he came upon a lion in great distress, having a fragment of bone caught in his throat (or between his teeth, as the Kanjur version has it). The Bodhisattva conceived the idea of placing a piece of wood as a prop between the lion's jaws, entered his beak far down the throat, loosened the fragment of bone and drew it out, then removed the wood prop. Having received thanks from the lion, he went his way.

Some time later, when he had been for a long time without suitable food, he came upon the lion feasting on the flesh of a freshly killed young antelope and asked him for a bit. "Is it not enough that thou art alive, after entering the mouth of a creature like me?" replied the lion. Thereupon the Great Being flew away upward to the sky. Some forest deity, indignant at the lion's affront, flew upward also and asked the Great Being why he had not torn out the lion's eyes and snatched a bit to eat. The woodpecker made him a little sermon on not giving way to anger because of the ingratitude of others. The deity eulogized him as "a holy ascetic knowing the future," and disappeared on the spot. (On the banner the scene begins at right center, and ends at right top.)

"In this manner, then, a virtuous person is incapable of betaking himself to wickedness, even though provoked, having never learned to do so. In this manner, a good nature being always striven for does not pass away, even when in the state of a beast."[34]

III

Tibetan Scriptures: the Kanjur and the Tanjur

Two GREAT collections of sacred texts, the Kanjur and the Tanjur, make up the Tibetan scriptures. They are as yet little known in the West. Only within the last fifty years have Western scholars examined Buddhist literature carefully. According to Evans-Wentz,

> No complete translations into any Occidental language exist either of the Pali canon of the Southern School or of the Tibetan canon of the Northern School. . . . European scholars have done little to advance knowledge of Northern Buddhism beyond indexing, or making outline analyses of the Tibetan canon and translating a very few portions of them. . . . The encyclopedic contents of the Tibetan canon are, therefore, unknown in any comprehensive detail, outside the monasteries of Tibet, Mongolia, China, Manchuria, and Japan. This is true, too, of the Chinese canon, called "The Three Treasures" (San Tsang).[1]

It is the Tibetan canon of the Northern School of Buddhism, called Mahayana, that concerns us here. The Northern School developed logically and philosophically out of the primitive Buddhism represented by the Southern School. It developed into a higher and in some respects an esoteric Buddhism, which extended salvation to the whole universe. It was called Mahayana for reasons explained by Waddell as follows:

> From its large capacity for easy, speedy, and certain attainment of the state of Bodhisat or potential Buddha, and conveyance across the sea of life, its adherents designated it "The Great Vehicle" or Mahā-yāna; while they contemptuously called the system of the others—the Primitive Buddhists, who did not join in with them—"The Little, or Imperfect, Vehicle," the Hinayāna, which could carry so few to Nirvana.[2]

For our knowledge of the Tibetan canon we owe much to two scholars: (1) to Alexander Csoma de Körös, for his analysis of the Kanjur and his abridgment of the subjects of discourse in the Tanjur, from a Narthang edition (the same edition has been used in the present text); and (2) to Léon Feer, who translated Csoma's English work into French and added an index.

The Kanjur

Kanjur (*bka-'gyur*) means "The Word Translated." The title in full is *rGyal-bai bka-'gyur rin-po-che* ("The Precious Translated Word of the Victorious One"—that is, Gautama, the Buddha). The Kanjur is the treasure-trove of the Buddha's teaching as it fell from his lips. His words were taken in by acute hearers. Every monk was supposed to remember the teaching as given, and able reciters gave the same teaching to others, who in turn became reciters. So, in an unbroken succession of reciters, the Buddha's words were handed down orally from generation to generation, until they were committed to writing in canonical form some four hundred years after the Buddha's death.

In its written form the Kanjur has seven great divisions:

1. *Dulva* (*'dul-ba*; Sanskrit *Vinaya*), i.e., "Discipline," in 13 volumes. This division deals with the education and training of those who adopt the religious life. It is interspersed, especially in the first four volumes, with Jatakas that skillfully show the importance of discipline in ordinary daily living.

2. *Sher-chin* (*sher-phyin*; Sanskrit *Prajñā-pāramitā*), i.e., "Transcendental Wisdom," in 21 volumes. This division deals with philosophical speculations or theories. It presents the psychological, logical, and metaphysical terminology of Buddhism, without settling on any determined subject, and abounds in abstract terms and definitions. The first 12 volumes contain the Prajnaparamita, in 100,000 stanzas (*shloka*'s), as translated from Sanskrit into Tibetan for the first time, in the ninth century A.D. Volumes 13-21 are abridgments of the Prajnaparamita. Volume 13, in 20,000 stanzas, is intended for monasteries or individuals who cannot buy the full text. Volume 16—a favorite with Tibetans, who hold it in special reverence—is intended for average or junior monks. One of the abridged volumes, titled "Transcendental Wisdom in a Few Letters," is a recension of three or four folios; it is intended for schoolboys and the laity. The whole Prajnaparamita is mystically condensed into "the letter *A*, the mother of all Tathāgatas and Buddhas." The letter *A* is considered the mother of all Wisdom, producing all Bodhisattvas and Buddhas, since *A* is the first element in forming syllables, words, or a discourse and provides the means of acquiring knowledge and wisdom.

The doctrine in these twenty-one volumes of "Transcendental Wisdom" was spoken, according to Tibetan texts, by Shakyamuni sixteen years after he became the Buddha—that is, in his fifty-first year. He delivered the doctrine on the mountain called Vulture Peak, near Rājagriha in Magadha, before a great number of Bodhisattvas and deities, and his own 5,000 disciples. Among these disciples were Śāriputra and Subhūti, whom the Buddha addressed principally, drawing them into asking questions which he did not answer directly but about which he formulated propositions such as would lead them to find their own solutions.

3. *Phal-chen* (*sans-rgyas phal-po-chen*; Sanskrit *Buddhāvatamsaka*), i.e., "Association of Buddhas," in 6 volumes. This division teaches morality and metaphysics by means of (1) descriptions of several Buddhas, their provinces, their great qualities, their ancient deeds for procuring the good of sentient beings, their praises, and many legends; and (2) enumeration of several Bodhisattvas, their different degrees of perfection, habits, and manner of living, and their wishes, prayers, and efforts for the good of all animated beings. These volumes tell how Shakyamuni made miraculous journeyings to influence a concourse of several Bodhisattvas to express themselves in regard to supreme being.

4. *Dkon-seks* (*dkon-brtsegs*; Sanskrit *Ratna-kūta*), i.e., "Jewel Peak," in 6 volumes. This division is an "enumeration of the diverse qualities and perfections of the Buddha and his teaching."

5. *Do-de* (*mDo-sde*; Sanskrit *Sūtranta*), i.e., "Aphorisms," "Axioms," or "Treatises," in 30 volumes. Some 270 treatises, on various subjects, are arranged throughout the volumes. The greatest part of these treatises show the moral and metaphysical aspects of Buddhism. They consist of legends about the lives of several individuals, with allusions to medicine, astronomy, astrology; stories to exemplify the consequence of acts done in former births; descriptions of orthodox and heterodox theories; moral and civil laws; accounts of the habitations of the six kinds of living beings, and the causes of their being born there; Buddhist cosmogony and cosmography, including the provinces of several Buddhas; and a picture of the exemplary life of any Bodhisattva. In general, all the twelve kinds of Buddhistic scriptures (discourses, exposition, verse, Jatakas, mysteries, etc.) are to be found in these volumes.

6. *Nyang-das* (*mya-ngan-las-'das-pa*; Sanskrit *Nirvāṇa*), i.e., "Deliverance from Pain," in 2 volumes. This division describes the death of

Shakyamuni, accompanied by great lamentation of all sorts of animated beings; their offerings and sacrifices to him; his teaching them, especially with regard to the soul; his last moments and funeral; how his relics were divided and where deposited.

7. *Gyut* (*rGyud;* Sanskrit *Tantra*), i.e., "Treatises," in 22 volumes. This division contains, in general, mystical theology, including "descriptions of several gods and goddesses; instructions for preparing *mandalas,* or circles, for the reception of those divinities; offerings or sacrifices presented to them for obtaining their favor; prayers, hymns, charms, etc., addressed to them"; also "some works on astronomy, astrology, chronology, medicine, and natural philosophy."[3]

In addition to the 100 volumes comprised in these seven divisions of the Kanjur, some editions have a volume containing an index and another containing supplements and corrections. The total number of volumes in the Kanjur varies from 100 to 108, depending on the edition.

The Tanjur

Tanjur (*bsTan-'gyur*) means "Translation of the Commentaries." The Tanjur is a great encyclopedic compilation of literary works, brought together, for the most part, by Indian pandits and learned Tibetans in the first few centuries after Buddhism had been introduced into Tibet in the seventh century A.D. Though closely linked up with the canonical Kanjur, the Tanjur is noncanonical, some of the subjects being even strange to Buddhism. (So Feer said in the Preface to his translation of Csoma's abridgment of the contents of the Tanjur.[4])

Totaling 225 volumes, the Tanjur has the following divisions: 87 volumes, the *rGyud* (Sanskrit *tantra*), deal with rituals and ceremonies; 136 volumes, the *mDo,* cover science and literature; 1 volume contains hymns to deities and saints; and 1 volume is an index. The first 16 volumes of the mDo are all commentaries on the Prajnaparamita of the Kanjur, followed by other commentaries and treatises on rhetoric, grammar, prosody, mechanics, and alchemy, and a Tibetan-Sanskrit dictionary of Buddhist terminology.

Compilation of the Doctrine

Colossal work went into the making of the 325 or so volumes of the Kanjur and the Tanjur. But preceding the colossal work of writing and printing the texts were centuries of oral presentations. Fortunately, there are records of how oral compilations were made.

Of the canon as it came to stand in the Kanjur—in its Mahayana, or Northern Buddhism, form—three compilations were made: The *first* was made immediately after the death of Gautama the Buddha. (Webster's New International Dictionary gives the date of his death as "?483 B.C."; Waddell gives it as somewhere between 477 and 370 B.C.) The *second* was made one or two hundred years (authorities differ) after the Buddha had died. The *third* was made during the reign of King Kanishka of North India, toward the end of the first century A.D., more than four hundred years after the death of the Buddha.

The *first compilation* of the doctrine took place in Magadha. The event is recorded in Volume 11 of the *Dulva* ("Discipline") division of the Kanjur. This is the only canonical version of the event found in Tibetan works, according to W. Woodville Rockhill, who translated it into English. The following account of this compilation is a paraphrase of Rockhill's translation:

The Buddha had just died. A concomitant circumstance of this event was the death of thousands of bhikshus (Sanskrit *bhikṣu*, an ordained monk; a mendicant ascetic). People remarked that, since thousands of bhikshus had died simultaneously with Śāriputra and Maudgalyāyana—the two greatest of the Buddha's disciples—and thousands more when the Buddha himself died, "the word of the Blessed One has vanished like smoke," there being no longer mighty bhikshus left to teach the Sūtranta, the Vinaya, and the Mātṛikā (Abhidharma) of the Blessed One. These remarks were heard by Mahākāshyapa, acknowledged head of the order because of his wisdom and virtues.

Mahākāshyapa decided to call an assembly of bhikshus, including 500 Arhats ("Venerable Ones") capable of working out what must be done, and to hold this important conclave in Magadha, where the Blessed One had acquired omniscience and where Adjatasatru, King of Magadha, being a firm believer, would provide the Brotherhood with necessaries. The king, on hearing of the announcement of the conclave, gave orders to supply everything required. The bhikshus then went to Rājagriha, and, casting about for a proper place, decided on the Nyagrodha cave (rightly, the Sattapani cave, by the side of the Webhāra mountain) as being sufficiently secluded for their purpose. The king provided the necessary bedding (mats). The 500 Arhats were examined to see if any one of them was still subject to passions, anger, ignorance, desire, or attachment.

The 500 requested Mahākāshyapa to preside over the assembly. Sitting in the lion's seat (pulpit), he asked them if they would allow Ānanda, beloved disciple of the Buddha, to begin the work of the council with the compilation of the *Sūtranta* ("sermons") of the Buddha. They consented by remaining silent—the traditional sign of acceptance—and then spread their cloaks over the pulpit.

Ānanda circumambulated the pulpit, keeping it to his right side, bowed down to the elders, and then sat down in the pulpit. He was thinking how he would recite the sermons chronologically, when Kāshyapa said to him: "Where did the Master, desiring the good of the world and having conquered (the Evil one), explain the chief dogmas? Recite the Sūtranta."

Having collected himself, Ānanda recited in a loud voice and with clasped hands the sermon of "The Establishment of the Kingdom of Righteousness"—in the very words spoken by the Buddha at Benares for the sake of the first five disciples, who had been at first bitterly opposed to him but were soon converted.

When Ānanda had finished, Adjnata Kaundinya, who had been one of those five, said: "Venerable Mahākāshyapa, I heard this sermon; it was spoken for my benefit. It dried my blood and the ocean of my tears. I left behind the mountain of bones; it closed the door of perdition, and opened for me the door of heaven and of freedom. When that precious jewel of a sutra was spoken, I and 80,000 devas acquired the clear eye of truth, and became free from sin (dri-ma). Now that I hear that sermon of long ago, I see that there is nothing which is not transitory!" And he fell senseless to the ground. Great also was the agitation of Ānanda and of all those present, as they thought of their dead Lord and that even he had not escaped the universal law of decay.

(Those first five disciples are strangely linked up with the "Feeding the Tigress" story, told in Chapter IV. They are supposed to have been the cubs in that story, in the version that gives the number as five, when they were saved by the Buddha in his far-past Bodhisattva existence. As he had saved them then, by giving his body to be eaten, so he saved them as men in this later existence by giving them spiritual food.)

Then Ānanda, as requested by Kāshyapa, recited the second sutra, which had also been spoken by the Buddha at Benares for the sake of those first five disciples. Kaundinya said that when he had heard it from the Buddha's lips it had made an Arhat of him and had converted his four companions; and again he fell senseless to the ground.

As Ānanda finished reciting each sutra, Kāshyapa and the assembly cried aloud, "This, then, is the dharma ("law"); this is the rule!" In this way Ānanda went through the whole sequence of the Buddha's sermons, thus establishing fundamentally this great Vessel of teaching.

Kāshyapa then proposed that "the venerable Upāli, a wise man, and one conversant with the origin of the rules and their history," should compose the Vinaya ("Discipline") part of the doctrine. The assembly assented.

Upāli had formerly been royal barber to King Śuddhodana, the Buddha's father. In that former time he had been sent to shave the heads and beards of the young Shākyas (Buddha's relatives) who were about to enter the order of the Blessed One; and when he had finished this work, he reflected that he would have entered the order himself, had he not had an "evil birth" (that is, birth in a lower caste). Standing near him was Śāriputra, one of the two greatest disciples, who, knowing that Upāli would become famous as a bhikshu, led him to the Buddha and said that Upāli wanted to enter the order. "Come hither, bhikshu," the Blessed One said, "and lead a life of purity." And "forthwith Upāli's hair fell off and he stood arrayed in bhikshu's apparel, an alms bowl in his hand, with the look of a bhikshu of eight years' standing."

Now, at the time of the conclave, Upāli became famous. He took his place in the pulpit. Having been asked by Mahākāshyapa where and for what reasons the first ordinance had been laid down by the Blessed One, Upāli replied that it was at Benares, on account of the five bhikshus, and that the Blessed One had ordained that "they should wear circular clerical garb (*chos-gos*)." He then narrated each rule and the circumstances attending it. The 499 other Arhats listened attentively and approved his words as the Teaching of the Master. Thus was established this great Vessel of teaching.

Then Mahākāshyapa thought that he himself would expound the Mātṛikā, to preserve the sense of the Sūtranta and Vinaya as spoken, "for the sake of those men who will hereafter wish for wisdom . . . and those who will delight in the essence (profound signification) of the doctrine." Thereupon, calling on the assembly to say in what the

Mātṛikā consisted, he made the compilation of the metaphysical parts of the doctrine.

"Then the yakshas above the earth cried out, 'Bravo! The venerable Mahākāshyapa and the 500 other Arhats have compiled the Three Baskets (*Tripiṭaka*) of the Tathāgata; the devas will swell in number, and the asuras will diminish! . . .'

"When the work of the council was over, Kāshyapa thought that as he had done all that was necessary for the preservation of the doctrine to future generations, his time had come to pass away; so he went to Ānanda and said to him, 'Ānanda, the Blessed One committed to my care the keeping of the doctrine, and passed away. Now, when I shall have passed away, thou shalt take care of the doctrine (i.e., be patriarch).'" He told Ānanda to whom he should confide the doctrine in his turn, and then went into preparation for his own *parinirvāṇa* (extinction of karmically conditioned existence; a State of Perfect Enlightenment).[5]

The *second compilation* of the doctrine took place in the time of the celebrated King Ashoka of the Maurya dynasty of Magadha, who "exercised authority more or less direct from Afghanistan to Ceylon," from about 234 to 198 B.C.[6] Converted early in his reign from the Brahmanical faith to that of the Buddha, he made Buddhism his State religion, maintained thousands of Buddhist priests at his palace, and erected thousands of pillars (topes) bearing inscriptions of Buddhistic import in Pali characters. In the eighteenth year of his reign, he held a great convocation of priests, which was followed by missions to Ceylon and other places. As writing seems certainly to have been in use in his day, it is probable that some of the scriptures were committed to writing.

The *third compilation* took place in the time of the much-disputed but also strongly vouched-for King Kanishka, with whom Śūra is supposed to have corresponded when composing his *Garland of Birth-*

Stories. It was toward the end of the first century A.D. that this Scythian king is said to have held the epoch-making council at Jalandhar in North India which declared the superiority of the Mahayana system (it extended salvation to the entire universe) over the Hinayana system (it confined salvation to a select few). Supporting the new doctrine with Buddhist zeal and munificence, King Kanishka published, in Sanskrit, versions of the Buddhist canon "from sources for the most part independent of the Pali versions of Southern Buddhists, though exhibiting a remarkable agreement with them."[7] He pushed the Mahayana system into becoming the dominant form of Buddhism throughout India and quickened its penetrating other countries, so that it is today represented by China, Mongolia, Tatary, Japan, Sikkim, Bhutan, Nepal, Ladakh, and Tibet.

Source and Format of Tibetan Scriptures

Tibetan scriptures are faithful translations from Sanskrit texts (a few are from Pali and Chinese texts) made by learned Indian and Kashmiri pandits and a few Chinese monks, with the assistance of Tibetan scholars. The earliest translations into Tibetan date to about A.D. 645. They were written in the time of Thon-mi Sambhota, who went to India to learn the art of writing (see Chapter I) and thus to make the spiritual treasures of Buddhist scriptures available to Tibetans. He invented an alphabet of thirty consonants and four vowels, and wrote eight works on grammar and writing. The greater part of the translations were made in the eighth and ninth centuries A.D., the ninth being the most prolific; and from the eleventh to the thirteenth centuries.

These sacred writings, holding in deposit the "Word" of the Buddha, are regarded by all Buddhists as forming the second member of the Trinity—that is, "The Three Most Precious Things" (*dkon-mchog gsum;* Sanskrit *Triratna*). The Buddha, as the originator of the Doctrine, is the first member; the corporate body of the priests, the third. These three—the Buddha, the Doctrine, the Brotherhood—constitute the mediators, with implications of supernatural power. In this Trinity, the pious Buddhist daily "takes his refuge" on his way to procuring highest perfection and holiness (*bodhi*). The books themselves are held materially sacred. They receive divine honors by being displayed in high places and worshiped with incense, lamps, and other emblems of religious rites.

The "books" are simply piles of unbound folios printed on both sides. Printing is done from hand-carved wood blocks. The paper is laid on the inked blocks, and an impression is taken by hand pressure and rubbing the back. Tibetans make a remarkably tough paper, resistant to moisture and vermin, from the inner bark of a shrub, *Daphne cannabina*, which comes from Nepal chiefly, from other parts of the sub-Himalayas, and from Chinese borderlands.

The folios are horizontally long and vertically narrow. Those of the Kanjur of the particular Narthang edition that was used in the present volume measure 22 x 6½ inches. Each folio of this edition has seven horizontal lines enclosed by a border. The Tanjur folios measure 22 x 4½ inches, and they also have seven horizontal lines. The characters of the Tanjur folios are smaller than those of the Kanjur. However, all characters of the Kanjur and Tanjur folios are fairly large, to enable monks to read in their dimly lighted monasteries.

Each volume has about 300 to 500 folios. Since they are printed on both sides, this would amount to from 600 to 1,000 pages. The sequence of folios is indicated by numbers, on the upper side, at the left.

Folios are laid on top of one another in numerical order. Then they are placed diagonally across a square of colored cloth, in which they are securely wrapped, with two of the ends tied the long way of the volume. Sometimes the folios are tied with cloth bands or leather bands. The wrapped folios are placed between two heavy wooden boards. (The folios of the edition of the Kanjur used in the present text are wrapped in a cloth of washed-red color, and the boards are painted a dull red.) A label printed on cotton or silk is put under one end of the top board, projecting slightly from it. Then the folios are stored, in order, in what Waddell calls "an open pigeon-holed rackwork."

Before opening a parcel of folios and also on rewrapping it, the reader-monk places the book reverently on his head, saying, "May I obtain the blessing of thy holy words!"

The first attempt to print the Tibetan canon, according to Kenneth K. S. Ch'en, "was made during the first part of the thirteenth century by a disciple of mChom-ldan-ral-Khri, who obtained funds from China for the purpose. The various masters . . . gathered together sutras, vinaya texts, and tantric texts from various places, collated and then printed them. Only then was the work (of putting the canon together) completed for the first time. This was known as the Snar-thang (Narthang) old edition."[8] It was named after the monastery where the work was done, about six miles from Tashi-lhunpo, capital of Western Tibet and headquarters of the Grand Panch'en Lama. Neither the wood blocks nor printed copies of the Narthang old edition are now available. In subsequent centuries other editions were printed from time to time: Lithang, Derge, Narthang new, Cone, Punaka, Rjes-rku-bum, Cha-mdo, Yung-lo, Wan-li, Peking, and Lhasa.

Carving the blocks of the Narthang new edition was begun by order of the seventh Dalai Lama in 1730. The Narthang old edition was used as the basic text, but the text was increased and supplemented by the catalogues of Tshal-pa sMon-lam-pa, Bu-ston Rin-po-che, and others. Tshal-pa was a Teacher who gave assistance in the founding of new monasteries in the twelfth century. Bu-ston brought the original copy of the bsTan-'gyur from Narthang, classified its texts, and added about one thousand new texts.

The cutting of the blocks alone required the services of eight hundred men. The work consumed one year and six months—from the twenty-sixth day of the eight month, 1730, to the twenty-sixth day of the first month, 1732, there being an intercalary month in between.[9]

An edition printed off these wood blocks, which are still stored at Narthang, was presented to the East Asiatic Library of Columbia University by Mr. and Mrs. Louis Horch. (This edition was made use of in the present volume.) The Kanjur of this edition is in 102 volumes (100 contain more than a thousand separate texts, one is an index, and one contains supplements and corrections), and the Tanjur is in 225 volumes.

It is in the Tanjur that the Tibetan translation of Ārya Śūra's *Jāta-kamālā* is found, in Volume 91 (or *ke*, as notated in the Tibetan fashion) of the mDo class, on folios 1-148; and on folios 149-375 is a commentary by Dharmakirti on thirty-two of Śūra's teaching stories. On the first and last folios of this volume are woodcut images such as are usually found in twos and threes on the beginning and end folios of distinctive divisions or volumes all the way through the scriptures. They depict Buddhas and Bodhisattvas, deities, great teachers, guardians, and other foremost upholders of Buddhistic teaching. Taken as a whole, from the first folio of the Kanjur through the last folio of the Tanjur, these images might well constitute an admirable, perhaps unique, Tibetan Buddhist pantheon.

Folio 1 of Tanjur Volume 91 of the mDo class is illustrated in Fig. 1. At the left end is an image of the Buddha, sitting in the lotus posture. His right hand is pendant, with knuckles to the front, in the "Earth-touching" or so-called "Witness" attitude (this alludes to an episode in which Shakyamuni, sitting under the "Tree of Wisdom," called the Earth to witness in his long and terrible temptation by Māra). The inscription that goes with this representation of the Buddha says "To the Highest of the Buddhas, adoration" (*thub-pai dbang-po-la na-mo*). The image at the right end represents Ārya Śūra. His right hand seems to be in the "Preaching" attitude. The inscription says "To Master Śūra, adoration" (*slob-dpon dpa-bo-la na-mo*).

» 84 «

FIG. 1. Folio 1, recto, of Volume 91 of the mDo division of the Tanjur. It is the beginning of Ārya Śūra's *Jātakamālā* as translated into Tibetan.

FIG. 2. The last folio, recto, of Volume 91 of the mDo division of the Tanjur.

FIG. 3. First folio, recto, of a gold-written manuscript copy of the Suvarṇaprabhāsottamasūtra.

Fig. 4. Second folio, recto, of the Suvarṇaprabhāsottamasūtra manuscript, showing two of the foremost among the Buddhas at the Vulture Peak gathering.

Fig. 5. Last folio, recto, of the Suvarṇaprabhāsottamasūtra manuscript. The four "Great Guardian Kings of the Quarters."

Fig. 6. Board cover of the Suvarṇaprabhāsottamasūtra manuscript. The Ranja characters are a pointed variety of the Devanāgari alphabet, used in Tibet and Nepal ornamentally in inscriptions and titles of books.

The four lines of text on Folio 1 are in the traditional beginning form of every separate text of Tibetan scriptures: "In the language of India, Garland of Birth-Stories. In the language of Tibet, chain of birth successions. Chapter the first." (In Tibetan: *rgya-gar skad-du/ dzā-ta-ka-mā-la/ bod skad-du/ skyes-pai rabs-kyi rgyud/ bam-po dbang-po*.) Then follows Śūra's "Salutation to the Highest of the Buddhas," whom he wishes to worship with his "handful of flowers."

The last folio of this Tanjur volume is illustrated in Fig. 2. Both the right and left ends show a chorten (*mchod-rten*)—a receptacle of offerings, corresponding to the chaityas and stupas, or topes, of Indian Buddhism. Chortens are usually solid conical masonry structures, the shape varying in different places and times. Originally, they were erected as sepulchers, intended to contain the relics of departed saints; later, as cenotaphs in honor (memory) of the Buddha or of deceased Holy Ones buried elsewhere. They are often seen in great numbers, especially near temples and convents; in such proximity they are looked upon as holy symbols of Buddhist doctrine.

The chortens in Fig. 2 show the Tibetan type, symbolic of the five elements into which a body resolves upon death. The lowest section, a solid rectangular block set on a stepped-up base, represents the solidity of *earth*. Above it is a globe, representing *water*. On this globe is a triangular tongue representing *fire*, made up of thirteen steplike segments, which stand for the thirteen Bodhisat heavens of the Buddhists. On the tongue of fire is a crescent—the inverted vault of the sky—representing *air*. And at the top an acuminated circle tapering into space—symbolic of the sacred light of the Buddha[10]—represents *ether*.

A chorten is described in the "Feeding the Tigress" story, told in two versions in Chapter IV. In the Dzanglun version the chorten is erected by the grieving family and friends for the remains of the young prince who had sacrificed his body to feed the starving tigress. In the Suvarṇa-sūtra version, it is the Buddha who, in teaching the Law of cause and effect, causes the same chorten to arise, *magically*, out of the earth on which it had long ago been erected, and to descend again into the earth as if sacredly preserved there.

✿

The latest edition of the Kanjur was ordered by the thirteenth Dalai Lama and printed at his press in Lhasa. The carving of the wood blocks, estimated at more than 30,000, was begun in 1920 and completed in 1927. The blocks are kept in a carefully guarded three-story building in Lhasa, directly across from the Potala, the Dalai Lama's palace. This Lhasa edition consists of 100 volumes (99 contain 1,086 texts, and one is an index).

The paper used was made up of several sheets of native paper pressed together with yak-hide glue, which gives a substantial surface on both sides for the thick black ink and thus avoids the blotting so commonly found in the Narthang edition. The clarity of the printing—and this is of considerable importance—is the main difference between this edition and other editions.

In checking some fifty Jatakas translated from the Narthang edition, which is sometimes referred to as the "standard" edition, with the same stories in the Lhasa edition, I found surprisingly few differences, mostly minor ones. But such correspondence might not hold true throughout the 99 volumes of texts.

The Dalai Lama, in presenting this Lhasa Kanjur to the Yale University Library as a gift, requested that its staff give the sacred volumes proper housing and care, and expressed his "personal wish and prayer that the Buddha's precepts in the Kanjur would illuminate the darkness like the radiance of the sun."[11]

✿

Manuscript copies of the scriptures, both as separate texts and as a whole, are innumerable. The earliest ones go back to the time when the doctrine was first committed to writing. Monks traveled from place to place to find texts needed for their own further enlightenment or for teaching. Wealthy and powerful rulers, who were ardent Buddhists and propagators of the Faith, had copies made of the whole body of Buddhist doctrine as it existed at their time.

Figures 3, 4, and 5 show folios from a manuscript copy of the Sublime Gold-Radiance Sutra (Suvarṇaprabhāsottamasūtra), which contains the "Feeding the Tigress" story.

This sutra was pronounced at Rājagriha on Vulture Peak—before the most distinguished audience, perhaps, ever to have been gathered together. Its nucleus was the Buddha's own full following, among whom were the five who first became his disciples, and Ānanda, the Beloved One. Mingling with them were all sorts of Buddhas and Bodhisattvas, deities, and demons: Licchavi Kumāras (mind-born sons of Brahma belonging to the Licchavi branch of the Shākya family); and the powerful four Great Kings of Space. All took an active part in the exalted meeting.

An attestation that accompanies the manuscript designates it as "the foremost of one hundred boxes of Tibetan" (that is, the Kanjur) caused to be "gold-painted, written by Royal order," during the reign of Ch'ien Lung, Manchu Emperor of China from 1736 to 1795. This emperor was a great administrator, a poet of some talent, and a patron of arts and crafts. He surrounded himself with distinguished philosophers, men of letters, and artists, who assembled the most immense anthology that ever came into being: 36,000 volumes, containing everything of value in Chinese having to do with Confucian classics. Each volume was copied seven times by hand. An ardent Buddhist, Ch'ien Lung had the Buddhist scriptures not only in Chinese but also in Tibetan, for he had the scriptures from the Tibetan copied. And his artists made sumptuous bronzes of the Tibetan pantheon.

The version of the Suvarṇaprabhāsottamasūtra that he had copied from the Tibetan had been translated from Sanskrit into Tibetan by the Indian scholars Jinamitra and Shīlendrabodhi, with the Tibetan Lo-tsā-ba Bande Ye-shes-de as Corrector, in the reign of Tibet's King Ral-pa-chan, A.D. 804-816. Ch'ien Lung must certainly also have had the version of this sutra that had been translated into Chinese (from a different Sanskrit original) by I-tsing, who died A.D. 713. I-tsing's Chinese version was translated into Tibetan by Bande Chos-grub, whose version is found in Volume 12 of the *rGyud* division of the Narthang edition of the Kanjur, together with the version translated directly from Sanskrit into Tibetan by the aforementioned Indian scholars.

The illustrations in Figs. 3 to 6 are from the manuscript copy of the Sanskrit-into-Tibetan translation. The 198 folios of this beautiful manuscript are gold-painted "written," on thick black paper with dark-blue borders. The folios measure 30 x 4½ inches. Each side of the folios has seven lines. On their pressed-down horizontal edges are fore-edge paintings. They present the eight glorious emblems, in color, four on one side, four on the other: the Golden Fish, Umbrella, Conch Trumpet, Lucky Diagram, Victorious Banner, Vase, Lotus, and Wheel. On the end edges are the *cintāmaṇi* ("wish-granting jewel") and the mystic syllable *Om*.

The first folio (see Fig. 3), framed in a yellow-and-green brocade-covered stiff backing, is veiled by a three-ply "curtain" of thin brocades: red lined with white, gray-green lined with blue, yellow lined with pink. Lifting these over the top edge, one sees, at the left, a beautiful image, in lacquered color, of Shakyamuni, in lotus posture, with the right hand in the "Earth-touching" or "Witness" attitude and the left hand holding the begging bowl, which attests detachment from all worldly things. At the right is Indra (*brGya-sbyin*), Lord of the Thirty-three (Devas), as a country-god (*yul-lha*), sitting on a lotus throne in "The Enchanter's (Mañjuśrī's) pose"; the right leg hangs down, inclining slightly inward, and the left is loosely bent. With both hands he holds his attribute, the conch trumpet, with which he calls together *"Die brahmanischen Götter zum buddhistischen Kult."*[12]

The traditional beginning, "In the language of India: Suvarṇa-prabhāsottamasūtra," appears on the upper side of the first folio. It is echoed on the second folio: "In the language of Tibet: *'phags-pa gser-'od dam-pa mdo-sdei dbang-poi rgyal-po zhes-bya-ba theg-pa chen-poi mdo.*" Both of these beginnings proclaim the sutra as "The Sublime Gold-Radiance Highest King of Indra-Sūtras Called—a Mahāyānasūtra."

The second folio (see Fig. 4) shows two images, in lacquered color, of Buddhas—portrayals, doubtless, of two foremost among the great number of Buddhas, from various corners of the world, present at the Vulture Peak gathering. Reverence is paid to them, severally, in the chapter on the Earth Goddess *brTan-ma* ("The Steadfast, or Firm, One"). As listeners to this "King of Sutras," they admire its excellence and pay homage to it. The Buddha at the right has his hands in "Best Perfection" attitude.

The last folio of this manuscript (see Fig. 5) is, like the first folio, framed and veiled in brocades. Pure illustration, it portrays the four "Great Guardian Kings of the Quarters," who defend the heavens from the attacks of outer demons. They visited the Buddha when he was in the Tushita heaven waiting for the time to come for him to manifest on earth. And they are supposed to have assisted him at every important event in his life—from receiving him at his birth "on the skin of a spotted tiger," to being present at his *parinirvāṇa.*[13] A whole chapter of the Suvarṇa-sūtra is devoted to their participation in the Vulture Peak gathering.

These four Guardian Kings are portrayed in Fig. 5 in the following order, reading from left to right:

1. The green, or blue, Guardian of the South, Virūḍhaka (*'phags-skyes-po*), King of the Khumbhaṇḍa (giant demons). Fierce-looking,

he clutches at his flaming beard, and in his hand he holds ready a lance-like sword, his symbol.

2. The white Guardian of the East, Dhṛitarāṣṭha (*yul-'khor-bsrung*), King of the Gandharvas (eaters of fragrance; musicians of the heavens). High-helmeted, with a plume from which ribbons hang, he plays on a stringed instrument, his symbol.

3. The yellow Guardian of the North, Vaishravaṇa (*rnam-thos-kyi-bu*), King of the Yakshas (supernatural beings who "injure," bring disease). With his right hand he holds the banner (of Victory) and in his left hand a mongoose—these being his symbols. In another aspect, he is Kuvera, the god of Riches.

4. The red Guardian of the West, Virūpākṣha (*mig-mi-bzang-rnams*), King of the Nagas (serpent gods). In his left hand he holds securely, close down against him, a red and twisting Naga. In his right hand, held high, is a chorten, symbol of the transitoriness of this life—a symbol that is dramatically exemplified in the tigress story, which is set jewel-like in this shining sutra.

❁

The whole make-up of this volume creates, for the magnificent sutra, an atmosphere of spiritual wonder. The sheaf of gold-written folios is wrapped in yellow brocade lined with red. The folios are held firmly in place between boards of satiny wood, which are tied by an inch-wide strip of velvety yak-hide with a dorje-chased buckle.

Carved on the boards (see Fig. 6) are the six mystic syllables *Om maṇi padme hūṃ* ("*Om*, the Jewel in the Lotus, *Hūṃ*"), in Indian Ranja characters of about the seventh century. The reciter of these syllables, which are endlessly repeated throughout Buddhist history, addresses Padmāpaṇi (Avalokita, Lord of Mercy), the patron god of Tibet, who controls rebirth and can convey the pleading one to where he no longer gives cause for the effect of his being born again and again.

If the suppliant's constant repetition of these mystic syllables does not bring this about, it does remind him of the inevitable working of the Great Law the Buddha put before his disciples—as revealed in the Jatakas that thread their way through the massive volumes of Tibetan scriptures.

IV

Feeding the Tigress

COMPASSION for all living beings, the basic virtue of Buddhistic life, is the essence of the famous tigress story in which the Bodhisattva, as a Brahman on his way toward Buddhahood, feeds his body to a starving tigress. It is with this story that Ārya Śūra opens his collection of thirty-four teaching stories of the former existences of the Buddha.

In Śūra's version, the Brahman is portrayed as an ascetic, with disciples about him; he goes with one of them, Ajita, into wild heights above his hermitage for meditation; there he is confronted with the opportunity "to be useful" (*phan-pa*) to such a degree as to make himself count to the utmost in that particular existence. In the Singhalese version, translated by R. Spence Hardy, the Brahman is described as follows: He was born in the village of Dāliddi and was named Brahma because of his great beauty. At sixteen he had read the three Vedas —Irju, Yaju, and Sama—and had become acquainted with all the sciences. He took up the "homeless life" near the rock Eraka, then called Mundi. Among his five hundred followers was one who stood out above all the rest: the Bodhisat one day to become Maitri Buddha.[1]

So impressed was Śūra with the Bodhisattva's gift of his own body to the tigress that "he thought he could do the same, as it was not so very difficult. Once he, as in the tale, saw a tigress followed by her young near starvation; at first he could not resolve on the self-sacrifice, but calling forth a stronger faith in the Buddha, and writing with his own blood a prayer of seventy slokas, he first gave the tigers his blood to drink, and when their bodies had taken a little force, offered himself." This statement, made in the Introduction to the *Jātakamālā*, was ascribed by Speyer to the Tibetan historian Tāranātha. Speyer commented that anyone who could compose such discourses as those of Śūra "must have been capable of himself performing the extraordinary exploits of a Bodhisattva."[2]

The tigress story was brought to the light of day in Europe in a Mongol grammar published at St. Petersburg in 1831. This grammar, by I. J. Schmidt, contained as reading exercises two accounts (translated by Schmidt from the Mongolian into German) of the story of the Bodhisattva giving his body as food to a hungry tigress to save the little ones she had just brought forth and was about to devour. Perhaps the story did not then have the success it would have obtained—as Léon Feer[3] commented in 1899—had it been published in a book other than a grammar, and a Mongol grammar at that. Since 1831 a number of authors have translated and analyzed texts of the story in Sanskrit, Tibetan, Chinese, Singhalese, and Khotanese. In 1845, Schmidt translated the story into German from the Tibetan of the Narthang edition of the Kanjur. However, the varying details in the different versions remained generally unknown until Feer gathered together the diverse recensions, collated them, and presented an ensemble as complete as possible of what he called a *curieuse légende*.

The story is known so far only from Sanskrit, Tibetan, Mongol, Chinese, Singhalese, and Khotanese texts. It is not in the great Pali collections of the Jatakas, nor in the Chariya-pitaka. It is found in two canonical works of the Kanjur: the *Damamūko*, or *Dzanglun*,[4] and the *Suvarṇaprabhāsottamasūtra*.[5] It is also found in two noncanonical works of the Tanjur: the Tibetan translation of Śūra's *Jātakamālā*[6] and Kshemendra's *Bodhisattvāvadānakalpalatā*.[7] And it is mentioned by Yuan Chwang (Hiouen Thsang), called "the Chinese Pilgrim."

Śūra begins his telling of the story by stating that he got it from his guru, "a venerator of the Three Jewels, an authority because of his thorough study of virtues, and beloved of his own guru by virtue of his religious practices."[8] The story as told by Śūra's guru must have been derived from the same source as the Singhalese version translated by R. Spence Hardy. In Śūra's version as in the Singhalese, the doer-of-the-deed is an ascetic sitting in a rock-set hermitage amid disciples. In the two Kanjur versions, as told by the Buddha, the Bodhisattva is a young prince, inordinately beloved by everyone because of his unusually tender behavior toward all beings.

The Dzanglun version is a true Jataka in form. It gives (1) the occasion on which the Buddha tells the story, having to do with the present; (2) the story of the past related to the present; and (3) the identification of the characters of the past with those of the present. The Suvarṇa-sutra version is basically the same as the Dzanglun in regard to characters and circumstances of the past, but it is told on a completely different occasion and is immensely expanded, being twice-told, in prose and in verse.

The Dzanglun version translated from Tibetan in the present chapter is from the Narthang edition of the Kanjur. It has been collated with the text of the Lhasa edition, from which it differs very little.

In rendering the Tibetan of these stories into English, I have attempted to keep close enough to a literal translation to get at the true meaning and at the same time to preserve the cadence and charm of the original.

The Dzanglun Story

The tigress story is the second chapter of the Dzanglun, or *The Sūtra Showing Various Examples of the Wise Man and the Fool.* This "Chapter of the Great Being's Having Given His Body to a Tigress" begins with the classic "These words were, at one time, heard by me," and continues:

The Victoriously Consummated One [Buddha] had his seat at Śrāvastī, in Jeta's park in the Garden-of-All-Joys (*ārāma*) of Anāthapiṇḍada. The time having come for collecting alms, the Bhagavant put on undergarment and clerical garb, took up his alms bowl and went with Ānanda [the Buddha's favorite disciple] to ask for alms.

In the town at that time, there was an old woman who had two sons, both of whom were continually stealing. Seized by a man of wealth (in the act of robbing him), they had been brought before the judge and, in conformity with the law, about to be executed, were now being led, bound, by the hangman to the place of execution.

Having seen from some distance the Bhagavant coming, the old woman and her sons made obeisance toward him, (she) saying: "O Chief among Deities! Look compassionately upon us, I beg of you, and save these my sons from being put to death!"

Thus she said. And the Bhagavant, having heard, out of great Tathāgata commiseration thought of them with heart-affection and, for the sake of saving their lives, gave order to Ānanda: "Request the king to let them go!" Thereupon the king, as requested, did let them go.

Great joy arose in them, and, mindful of the kindness of the Bhagavant, they betook themselves to where he was, made salutation with crown of head at his feet, folded together the palms of their hands, and thus besought him: "As our lifetime, by the great favor of the Bhagavant has become now but a remnant, O Chief of Deities, look compassionately upon us and allow us to take holy orders. Thus we beg."

At the Bhagavant's uttering "You are welcome!," hair of head and beard fell of itself from them and their garments became the color of saffron [the color of priestly robes]. When their believing spirit had made itself steadfast, they were taught by the Buddha whatever religious understanding was possible for them; and, ridding themselves of dust and impurity, they became Arhants [worthy ones; venerable ones; the most perfect Buddhist saints]. Their old mother, also, by hearing the Doctrine, became One-Who-Does-Not-Return-Again (Anāgāmin).

Seeing, at that time, such extraordinarily wonderful occurrences, Ānanda exclaimed in praise: "How many are the accomplishments of the Tathāgata!" Further, to himself he thought: "By these three, the old woman and her two sons, what good thing was done formerly that now, having met with the Bhagavant, they have been freed from great calamity and obtained the happiness-of-having-passed-away-from-affliction (Nirvāṇa)? With one body (in one life-period) obtaining blessing and happiness! Excellent!"

Knowing what Ānanda was thinking, the Bhagavant said to him: "Not only now have I kept alive these three, mother and sons; but earlier, in time passed away, by my kindness I preserved them."

"How," Ānanda besought him, "in earlier passed-away time did the Bhagavant keep these three, mother and sons, alive, I beg him to explain."

THEN THE BHAGAVANT TOLD ĀNANDA:

"Formerly, in time passed away, innumerable Kalpas ago, there was on this earth a king, Mahāratha (Great Vehicle), so called, ruling over five thousand feudatory princes. That king had three sons: the eldest, Mahāpraṇāda (Great Voice), so called; the middle one, Mahādeva (Great Lord), so called; the youngest, Mahāsattva (Great Being), so called. That youngest son, kind and compassionate from infancy, behaved toward all as to an only son.

"One day, while the King, with his ministers, his consort, and his sons, was resting a little during the course of taking a walk outside (the city), the three sons went on into a grove, where they saw a tigress, who, having whelped, tormented for many days by hunger and thirst, was on the point of eating her offspring.

"The youngest prince said to his two elder brothers: 'This tigress is indeed pressed by great affliction, exhausted, emaciated, and so near death as to come to eating the offspring she has brought forth.'

"'What you say is the truth,' the two elder brothers answered.

"'This tigress, what does she eat for food?' the youngest brother asked the elder ones.

"'With just-killed fresh flesh and warm blood, she becomes satisfied,' they answered.

"'Is there anyone,' the youngest brother pursued, 'suitable because of (having) such a natural body as to preserve the life of this one, able to act unqualifiedly?'

"'There is, indeed, no one,' the two elder brothers answered, 'because of its being so very difficult.'

"Then that youngest prince thought to himself: "For a long time, turning round in the orb of transmigration, wasting body and life untold times, sometimes because of passion, sometimes because of hatred, sometimes, indeed, because of stupidity, having given over my body, what worth is there to this body which not even for one time on behalf of religion has met with the region of virtue?'

"Thinking thus, while the three went along together, he said after a time to his two elder brothers: 'My two elder brothers, go on ahead! I, having attended to some business, will come along later.' Having thus spoken, he started (back) on that very same way; and, going quickly to where the tigress was, lay down before her. But her mouth was so closely shut that she could not eat him. Then the prince, by means of a sharp splinter of wood, brought forth blood from his body and gave the tigress opportunity to lick it, (whereupon) she opened her jaws and ate the flesh of his body without there being anything left of it.

"The two elder brothers, seeing after a long time that he did not come, turned back to search for him, meditating about the afore-mentioned grove,[9] 'Undoubtedly, the hungry tigress has killed him.'[10]

"Having arrived there, they looked around and saw that their young brother had been eaten by the tigress, the earth everywhere being stained with his flesh and blood so as to be most unclean. Losing conscious-ness, they fell to the ground. After a long time, recovering breath, they uttered lamentations, rolling about upon the ground, again faint-ing away.

"Meanwhile, the Queen Mother, in a dream saw three pigeons, among whom the smallest one, while they flew about frolicking, was carried away by a falcon. Directly upon awakening from the dream, terrified, she told it to the King. 'A pigeon, as I have heard said, is the soul of a son. In its being the smallest one that was carried away, of a certainty, to the most beloved of my sons a misfortune has happened.'

"Searchers were at once everywhere sent out, and soon after came the two princes. 'The beloved of my sons,' the Queen asked them, 'is he unhurt? Where is he?'

"The two elder brothers, words sticking in their throats, for a long time not even getting breath, were unable to speak. With breath returning, they said: 'He has been eaten by a tigress!'

"Hearing those words, the Queen, losing consciousness, fell to the ground. On her coming to herself, after a long time, the King, with his two sons, his consort, and the palace retinue, went to the place where the prince had 'changed life' (died).

"Meanwhile, the prince's flesh had been completely eaten by the tigress, and they saw only the ground stained with his blood and strewed with his bones. The Queen took up the head (skull) and the King the hand (bones), lamenting and weeping, and there they, again having lost consciousness, came to themselves after a long time.

"That Prince Mahāsattva, there having 'changed life,' was born again in the 'joy-possessing-region of the Devas' (Tushita heaven). He thought: 'Why, and because of accomplishing what deed, have I been born here?' Looking about with the 'eye of Deity' everywhere throughout the five Natures (realms of beings), he saw in the grove the small bones of himself that had 'changed life,' attended by his father and mother wailing and lamenting in torment of misery because of their loving him so much.

"Then the Deity thought: 'On account of my father and mother's being so very unhappy, in case that harm might come to (their) body and life, to encourage them I shall go and speak to them.'

"Having so thought, he moved downward from the sky, and from the heights above them he caused joy to arise in them with all sorts of endearing speech. His father and mother, looking up toward the sky, said: 'O Deity! Who are you? Tell us!'

"The Deity answered: 'I am, indeed, Prince Mahāsattva, so called. Because of giving my body to a hungry tigress, I was born again in the Deva region. Great King, act to understand in this way:

" 'Things, however much desired, finally perish.
In becoming, one of a certainty disappears.
In having sinned, one falls into hell-places.
In acting virtuously, one is born again in the Heavens.
In its being the lot of all to arise and to pass away,
Why, for the sake only of being joyful,[11] do you not perceive
The falling down into the sea of affliction?
Strive diligently for virtuous things!'

"Thereupon his parents said: 'You, indeed, out of great kindness fed the tigress, being compassionate toward all. Us having forsaken by fulfilling your time of life (by dying), we, indeed, because of thinking of you, are tormented by affliction as much as if our flesh were cut into pieces! Practicing great compassion by acting in such a way, is that right?'

"Then—that Deity appeasing them by means of all sorts of sweet-sounding words, by his own rejoicing also a little joy arising to his parents—they made a casket of seven kinds of jewels, laid his bones within it, and over the hidden coffer erected a chorten. The Deity went back again into his region, and the King and his retinue went back, also, to the palace."

To Ānanda, the Bhagavant said:

"In your mind, what think you? At that period of time, King Mahāratha, who do you think he was? Now, indeed, he is my father, King Śuddhodana. The King's consort at that time is now my mother, the beautiful lady Māyā. The eldest son at that time, Mahāpraṇāda, is (now) Maitreya. The middle son, Mahādeva, is (now) Vamisutra (Vasumitra). As to the youngest prince, at that time Mahāsattva, think none other but I am he. The tiger young ones of that period are now these two men whom formerly, long ago, I freed from evil, saved from execution, and made happy. Now (having become) manifestly Buddha, having acted to free them from an evil spirit, I delivered them completely from the great affliction of transmigration."

At that time, Ānanda and all the many followers (of Buddha) praised openly the words of the Buddha.

The Suvarṇaprabhāsottamasūtra Story

In the Suvarṇaprabhāsottamasūtra,[12] the occasion for telling the tigress story follows—indeed, is apparently induced by—the telling of another story by the Buddha. This other story illustrates the working of cause and effect. It is told before the Bodhisattva Vṛkṣadevatā and her ten thousand "sons" (disciples), in whose region the Buddha is wandering with his own following.

These "sons" of hers, formerly fishes in her region when she had been the Kuladevatā (the Bodhisattva Samuccayā), he (the Buddha)—at that time a great physician, Jalavāhana—helped her to save by adroitly getting water and food to them in a period of killing drought. He tells them that not only, in that long-passed-away time, as one practicing the life of a Bodhisattva, had he, by providing water and food, saved the life of those fishes (cause) now here as disciples (effect) on their Bodhisattva way, but (striking the new chord) "for the sake of being useful to other Bodhisattvas, my own body even I gave over. I will act to make further seen what cause and effect are."

Making, then, many hundreds of thousands of rays of light shine forth from openings in the world in the ten directions above and below the seat of the Bodhisattva goddess, as if to light up magnificently the way toward the new stage, surrounded by the thousands of followers of the goddess and attended by his own thousand Gelongs, he proceeded with obvious intent on into the Pāñcāla country. There, coming to a great forest on very level ground without thorns—green and tenderly spread everywhere with beautiful sacred sweet-scented flowers and soft grasses—the Buddha said to Ānanda: "Spread my mat for me near this tree!"

Ānanda, having obeyed, obviously feeling the heavily charged atmosphere, besought him: "Bhagavant, make us to understand the meaning (of all this)!"

The Buddha, having assumed the cross-legged posture upon the mat, making straight and erect his body, and having entered into make-use-of-real-memory, said to the Gelongs: "Do you wish to look upon the relics of the former body of a Bodhisattva formerly practicing penance?"

"We do indeed wish to behold them!" answered the Gelongs.

Then the Buddha, with his hand, highly ornamented with a hundred meritorious actions, possessing signs and symmetries, struck upon the ground. At the same time the great earth was shaken in six directions; the ground, bursting asunder, opened up; and a chorten made of seven kinds of jewels, greatly ornamented with a network of all sorts of precious things, rising up, emerged, and, on being seen by all the many attendants, brought about the arising of thoughts of greatest astonishment.

Then the Bhagavant, having arisen from his mat, made reverence to the chorten, circumambulating it to the right, and, again sitting down on his mat, said to Ānanda: "Open the door of this chorten!"

Ānanda opened it; and, seeing a small box made of seven kinds of precious stones, ornamented with most excellent sacred things, said to the Buddha: "Bhagavant, a small box made of seven kinds of jewels, ornamented with various precious things, is there."

"Open the box!" the Buddha ordered.

Obeying, Ānanda saw relics of snow-white color and like unto white lotus flowers. He said to the Buddha: "Inside the box, relics of pure color, distinguished most particularly from others, are there."

"Bring here the bones of a Great Being!" said the Buddha.

Having taken up the relics, Ānanda gave them over to the Buddha; and the Buddha, receiving them, said to the Gelongs: "Arrange the relics of a Bodhisattva practicing penance and look upon them!"

Then he said in verses:

"Bodhisattva mind possessing best qualities,
  By great bravery and exertion accomplishing the six pāramitās,[13]
  Always meditating for the sake of bodhi, uninterruptedly,
  Great thought of renouncing steadfast in mind, without wearying.

"GELONGS: All of you, with reverence bow down before the body of a former Bodhisattva! These relics, perfumed completely with the odors of religious duties, with samadhi and wisdom, because of being the most excellent pure region of meritorious actions, are very difficult to meet with."

Then the Gelongs and the many attendants, with collected mind, palms laid together, head touching the relics, paid such reverence as never before had been paid. Thus were praises uttered.

Ānanda then asked the Buddha to explain the relation of those bones to cause and effect.

"I am the cause of those bones," the Buddha replied, proceeding then to tell the story of himself as the young prince giving his body to the tigress.

In this version the king was accompanied only by his sons when he went out from the city to refresh himself with seeing the forests and hills. The sons, wandering on ahead to look for flowers and fruits, came to a bamboo grove, where they rested. (Their conversation is very different from that of the Dzanglun version.)

The eldest brother said, "Today my mind has become frightened. In this forest here, might we not be killed by pernicious wild animals?" The middle brother said that from the very beginning he had never cared about saving his own body; his apprehension here was the arising of a feeling of affliction from the possibility of being separated from those dear to him. The youngest said, "This, indeed, is a place of the coming together of deities and hermits. To me there is no uneasiness concerning fears for body or of being separated from anyone, since my body and mind are all filled with rejoicing rising up at the coming to the obtaining of sublime accomplishment."

They went on into the grove, where they saw the tigress with *seven* cubs about her. The eldest prince, describing her state, declared that she would certainly devour her offspring. At the young prince's asking what she usually ate (the talk about procuring suitable food for her is similar to the talk in the Dzanglun, with the young prince asking if there is anyone who would give his own body for that purpose), the eldest said, "Among all things difficult to give up, nothing is more difficult than (giving up) one's own body."

The young prince said: "Today we, each for himself attached to his own body, manifestly taken up with it and without wisdom, are not able to be useful to others; but holy men (saints), because of having greatly compassionate minds, despising their own bodies for the sake of being continually useful to others, act to benefit living beings." Further, he thought to himself, "This body of mine, for hundreds of thousands of existences without there being any profit from it, having been thrown away, rotten and putrefied, why today do I not think of acting to remove the misery of one pressed by hungers?"

Then they resumed their wandering onward, the young prince thinking to himself: "Today is the time for me to give over body and life. For a long time this body has been held onto by me, impure, foul, unpleasing in mind, with necessaries, clothing, food, vehicles, elephants, horses, wealth, and precious offerings even made for it. Coming up and passing away things are. I myself (am) not durable, continually seeking, difficult to be satisfied, very difficult to watch over." On and on his thoughts went, regarding his body not as useful but, indeed, as an enemy.

Thereupon his thoughts turned to action: "Today, with this body of mine, having accomplished manifestly a deed of wide and great extent, having equipped a great vessel on the sea of birth and death, having wholly renounced the orb of transmigration, of a certainty I will act to obtain deliverance." Further and further he wove the texture of his emancipation from all the distresses of life that having a body entails, until, uttering a wishing prayer, with thought of great compassion, mind grown stout, he told his elder brothers to go on ahead, and he would come later.

Returning to the bamboo grove, he approached the tigress. He took off his clothes, hung them on a bamboo branch, and then uttered his final wishing prayer:

"I, indeed, experienced in religion, for the sake of all living beings,
To say nothing of acquiring very highest bodhi sphere,
Having arisen in me mind of great compassion, unshakable,
Act to give away a body spared by human beings,
In bodhi health, without being pained,
Greatly esteemed by all possessed with understanding.
May all living beings in the great sea of affliction, in the three regions,
Remembering me today, be caused to pass into a happy state!"

Having uttered these words, the young prince lay down before the tigress. But "because of the power of the brightness of his compassion," the tigress was unable to do anything. Seeing her thus, the prince climbed a high hill nearby and threw himself down, thinking, "This tigress because of exhaustion is unable to eat me." On this thought he got up to search for a cutting instrument. Not finding one, he took a splinter of dry bamboo, causing with it blood to flow, and slowly neared the tigress.

As by the wind the rivers are shaken, so the great earth became shaken in six directions, the sun became darkened, and, everywhere in the ten directions close darkness having come, the gods caused a rain of sacred flowers and holy perfume filling and heaping the whole grove. The god assemblages of the region of atmospherical space, seeing such occurrences arising as never before they had seen, with mind rejoicing, afterward declaimed: "It is a Great Saint! (Mahāpurusha!) Excellent!" and continued to praise him in verses.

Meanwhile the tigress, seeing the blood flowing from the young prince's neck, having managed to lick it, ate the flesh of his body without there being anything left.

The elder brother, having seen the shaking of the earth, the darkness, the rain of flowers filling the sky, said to the middle one, "These certainly are signs of the young one's having given his body to the tigress!" With the middle brother, who seemed doubtful, he went back to the lair of the tigress, only to see the young one's clothes hung over the bamboo branch, and bones and hair scattered everywhere.

Mourning wildly together, asking each other what they could say to their parents, who loved the young one so much, weeping and lamenting, they finally gave up and went toward home.

During this time the attendants of the young prince, having lost all track of him, were making search, asking back and forth where he could be; and the Queen Mother, back in the palace, was having a dreadful dream with ominous signs—young pigeons (as in the Dzang-lun version) and the cutting off of her breasts—awaking to direful manifestations in the shaking of the earth, with everything trembling in unison, great forest trees and rivers, the sun darkened, her own eyes wavering, her heart as if struck by an arrow. And now the inner retinue of female attendants reported to her that the outside retinue of men had not found the prince. Certain that he was lost, she went to the King, who endeavored to cheer her up, saying that they would go together to seek him.

They went forth, then, from the city, together with many assemblages of people starting out, each for himself, in all directions, searching. Soon the chief minister came to the King, saying that he had heard the young prince was not alive. Great lamenting took place, during which the second minister came, so broken by what he had heard that he could say nothing. Lamentation mounted until finally the second minister was able to make clear definitely that the young prince had given over his body. On this baldly made expression of the young prince's fate, the King and Queen, in the height of frenzy, hurried to the bamboo grove, where they saw scattered everywhere bones and hair. In uttermost depths of despair, they lost consciousness, falling to the ground. Sprinkled with water by the great minister and other attendants, they came to themselves only once more to lament, hands uplifted, beating their breasts, weeping. Going over and over her dream, in repetitive detail, the Queen imploringly asked who could have so cut him in pieces. When she had become somewhat quieted, that great King and she and the two sons, joined together in love, took off all their ornaments, weeping, and, together with the many assemblages, having gathered up the relics of the Bodhisattva's body for the sake of making an offering, placed them within a chorten.

Here the story itself was finished, but the Buddha went on to speak of cause and effect in his own life, and then he began the tigress story again, telling it this time in verse. In the verse form he compressed the story more tightly, as if to incise it on the minds of his listeners, and put great emphasis on the lamenting.

In concluding verses he named the characters and identified them with characters of the past. (The names given by the Buddha on this occasion differ somewhat from those in the Dzanglun.) He named the middle prince as Mañjuśrī (instead of Vasumitra); the tigress as Mahāprajāpatī, the Buddha's aunt and foster mother. Of the seven tiger cubs (instead of two as in the Dzanglun), he said that five were now his first five disciples; the other two, the great Śāriputra and Maudgalyāyana.

At the end the Buddha summed up his experience of having finally accomplished bodhi:

> "By me, to all of you, has been set forth
> My being useful formerly to others
> As Bodhisattva behavior.
> The cause of accomplished bodhi has been taught,
> By the Bodhisattva's uttering at the time of giving up his body
> The words of the great wishing prayer:
> 'May I, by my body's remaining bones
> Be useful to living beings not yet come!'

> "This being the place of the body's having been given,
> That chorten made of seven kinds of jewels
> Remained here, meanwhile, innumerable years,
> Then from below the earth came forth

By power of the former wishing prayer.
The effect, how it is, tell living beings.
For being useful to gods and men,
Forth out of the earth it became raised up."

While the Buddha put forth this dissertation to innumerable assemblages of deities and of men, complete love and great rejoicing arose such as had never before arisen. Having uttered praises, all turned their minds toward "highest really accomplished bodhi." Then the Bhagavant—having said to the Bodhisattva Vṛkṣadevatā, "For the sake of showing myself grateful, I have paid respect with devotion"—manifestly collected the magical appearances back into himself, and the chorten again sank below the earth.

The tigress story in the Tibetan text of the Suvarṇa-sūtra edited by Johannes Nobel[14] presents on the whole the same account. He used several editions of the Kanjur other than the Lhasa edition used in the translation in the present chapter. It is only in lesser details (such as five cubs instead of seven) that a considerable number of variations occur. The text edited by Nobel ends with the Buddha's recalling the wishing prayer he had made as the young prince, for being useful to living beings in time to come, and finally declaring: "This chorten here is, indeed, the cause of the teaching (I have been giving you). The effect, indeed, it is." Whereupon that chorten, with the blessing of the Buddha, entered within the same spot where it had arisen.

That spot was given an exact location by Yuan Chwang (Hiouen-Thsang), who has been called "the Chinese Pilgrim." In his memoirs, written in the seventh century A.D., he placed it at 200 li (66 miles?) southeast of the Indus River where one crosses to the heights of the northern frontiers of the Kingdom of Takshaśila, and described it as being marked by a great gate of stone "at the place where the Prince Royal, Mahāsattva, abandoned his body to feed a starving tiger." At

140 or 150 steps from this gate (as Feer[15] tells it from the account given in Yuan Chwang's memoirs), there is a chorten in stone at the spot where the Great Being pierced his body with a piece of dry bamboo and nourished the tiger with his blood.

The "piece of dry bamboo" is designated as "a sharp thorn" in Thomas Watters' *On Yuan Chwang's Travels in India, 629-645 A.D.* And Watters took his description of the "spot" from Yuan Chwang's memoirs when he wrote: "The soil and the vegetation of the spot had a red appearance as if blood-dyed. Travellers suffering from the wild thorns of the place, whether they are believers or sceptics, are moved to pity."[16]

Of the chorten, Watters wrote: "The tope near the 'grave' or spot in which the Mahāsattva's bones were interred was known as the Sattva-śarira Tope, or 'tope of the relics of the Bodhisattva having given up his body to the tigress.'" It was believed to have been built by the King of Gandhāra "after he had heard the pathetic story from the Buddha." Continuing to describe the spot according to the Memoirs, Watters wrote: "To the north of the body-offering tope was a stone Ashoka tope about 200 feet high with very artistic ornamentation and shedding a miraculous light. Small topes and above 100 small shrines encircled the grave; pilgrims afflicted with ailments made circumambulation, and many were cured. To the east of this tope was a monastery with above 100 Brethren, all Mahāyānists."

Thus is witness borne to the place where the tigress story was enacted.

Records of the Tigress Story in Medieval Art

In far-flung places to which the teaching of Gautama, the Buddha, penetrated, the story of his former birth as Prince Mahāsattva has been conserved in paintings on medieval temple walls and shrines, in sculptured reliefs, and on Tibetan tankas.

The *Tigresse Affamée*, illustrated in Fig. 7, is painted on the lacquer of a shrine in the Buddhist Hōryūji Temple, Nara Province, Japan. It dates from the eighth century A.D. This painting portrays the young prince near the edge of the cliff he has ascended for his purpose, reaching up to hang his garment on a bamboo limb, and, in complete relinquishment, letting his body slip through the air in zephyrlike descent. Having reached the ground, he lies at one with the earth, offering his body in self-abnegating compassion. The starving tigress feeds hungrily on his bounty; the cubs, too, one even nuzzling at his unresisting outstretched arm.

Another place in which paintings of this scene appear is in the ruins of temple caves in East Turkey, near Kutscha, especially in Qyzil. These paintings probably date from the seventh century A.D. Again and again the same scene appears on the walls of these temple caves—in friezes which picture Jatakas and Avadanas. Four sketches and two photographs of such temple-cave paintings are shown in Figs. 8 to 13. With naïve charm, they depict the leap being made, the body bounty being given by the Bodhisattva.

The sculptured scene in Fig. 14 is carved on the base of one of the two broad-set, two-storied granite towers erected in Zayton, China, during the Sung and Yuan periods in A.D. 1228-50 and known as "The Twin Pagodas of Zayton." A book bearing this title, by G. Ecke and F. Demiéville, provided the illustration for Figure 14.

Zayton is the ancient name (it survives in our word "satin") of Ch'üan-chou in the province of Fu-chien. In the thirteenth century, it was one of the greatest harbors in the world and a center of foreign trade; it imported "the most astonishing quantity of goods and of precious stones and pearls"[17] and exported pepper and other spices; it was visited by Marco Polo and other famous travelers, and by rich and powerful traders.

The carving shows the lair of the tigress after she has eaten the

FIG. 7. *Tigresse Affamée.*

FIG. 8. Sketch of painting from the Cave of the Choir of Musicians.

FIG. 9. Painting from the Cave of the Sword-Bearer.

FIG. 10. Sketch of painting from the Cave of the Ravine.

Fig. 11. Sketch of painting from the Cave of the Prayer Mills.

Fig. 12. Sketch of painting from the Cave of the Manuscripts, ruins of Šorčuq.

Fig. 13. Painting from the Cave with the Bodhisattva Vault.

Fig. 14. Tigress, with cub and bones, and the Bodhisattva's clothes hanging over a limb.

prince. It is the scene that the two brothers beheld when they returned to the grove (as told in the Suvarṇaprabhāsottamasūtra version of the story) to see what had become of their beloved young brother. His garment hangs, like a banner of victory, over the bamboo limb. A lively cub is there, saved from being eaten by its mother, who, now strongly on her feet again from the feast of princely flesh, is worrying the residue of bones. The carving even shows the splinter of bamboo used by the prince to make his blood flow forth in order to entice the exhausted tigress to eat—accenting the perfection of the compassionate deed.

V

Three Jatakas from the Kanjur

IT WAS IN the monastery garden of Nigrodha, at Kapilavastu, his birthplace, that the Buddha told the three stories translated in the present chapter. He had been absent seven years. His father, King Śuddhodana, had sent many contingents of emissaries to persuade his son, Gautama, become the Buddha in those absent years, to return to see his kinsmen and let them profit by his teaching. When finally the Buddha, having consented, was actually on the way, the king prepared the Nigrodha garden for his reception, with a throne to sit upon. A great procession was sent to meet him.

Yet there was unwillingness on the part of the elders of the family to worship him as the Buddha on his arrival. Opposition persisted until the Buddha overcame it by magical means, such as rising in the air and sending forth colored rays of light to show his higher powers. (This demonstration is described in the Singhalese version translated by R. Spence Hardy.[1])

One member of his family, however, remained adamant. This was his cousin and brother-in-law, Devadatta, who had been jealous of him from childhood. Now that the Buddha had returned home as a great teacher, Devadatta proceeded to set himself up as a rival, with 500 disciples in his own vihara. Not only did he try to attract to himself disciples of the Buddha, but made attempts to injure him bodily, even to bring about his death.

The Buddha exposed his archenemy in a series of stories of the past in which Devadatta showed himself continually ungrateful, no matter how kind the Buddha was to him.

These are true Jatakas, in which the past struggle between Yes and No is set against an occasion in the present. They illuminate the NOW in each one's inner state of being—that NOW so precariously underlaid by past deeds and opened to future deeds.

As told in the Kanjur by the Buddha himself, these three stories of Devadatta and the Buddha show many interesting differences from the versions given by Ārya Śūra. Whatever original sources Śūra called upon for the essentials of his high, poetical teaching, he obviously modeled the material to give moral emphasis to the working of the law of cause and effect as fixing one's lot in the future (*karma*). The Buddha told the stories in simple fashion—as happenings in which constant inner effort manifests itself in ever higher ways of acting—bringing them close to daily life.

The Buddha as a Deer, Called Goldenside

The Buddha told the story of the deer Goldenside (Śūra's "Ruru Deer," but the two versions differ greatly) after he had told the following story of himself in a former existence:

While living as a hermit in an uninhabited region, he had come upon a baby elephant, just born, abandoned by its mother on her having heard a lion roar. He reared the elephant, but, despite all his care in cleaning, feeding, and watering it, and all his efforts to train it to proper conduct, it grew into a greater harassment with every increase in stature. It tore up flowering bushes, stripped fruit trees, and committed a thousand other harmful acts. The hermit was compelled to reprimand it more and more severely, which resulted only in its becoming more violent. At last it rushed at him with intent to kill, so that he had to break through the wall of his hut and flee.

That elephant, who was so "ungrateful and did not perceive it" was now Devadatta, he explained to his disciples. Devadatta had just been benignly cured by the Buddha after having eaten a great deal too much butter for him to digest—thirty-two ounces, to be exact. He had eaten all this butter in emulation of the Buddha, who could easily assimilate such a large amount because, as the physician who had prescribed it for him said, he had a "diamond body." Though all the Gelongs, with their own eyes, had seen the cure performed, Devadatta stubbornly denied it, saying that all by himself he had finally got to the point where he digested the butter.

This stubbornness supplied the occasion for initiating the series of stories—starting with the elephant story—about Devadatta as an ungrateful being, in one form or another, in past lifetimes. Each time, though befriended by the Buddha, he kept on being ungrateful and doing ever greater harm. And each time, not perceiving his own ungratefulness, even with jealous eyes upon the one pursuing his Bodhisattva-way upward toward freedom, he let himself slip over edge after edge down the slope into the chasm that ends in the dreadful hell Avīci, where, befriended still by the Buddha, he might, after long torment, start his way upward again.

"How, at another time, this one was ungrateful and did not perceive it, listen!" is the repeating link in the chain of life stories that prepared the way for the Buddha's telling of the existence in which he was the deer Goldenside.[2] (See Tanka A, Plate XIV. Tanka A illustrates the

Tanka A

Winning mercy for the creatures
Saving the monkey troop
Manifesting forbearance

PLATE XIV

The progression of scenes is described in the birth-stories of Chapter II. (*a*) "Winning mercy for the creatures," twenty-sixth birth succession. (*b*) "Saving the monkey troop," twenty-seventh birth succession. (*c*) "Manifesting forbearance," twenty-eighth birth succession.

Tanka B

Perfection of giving

PLATE XV

The whole story of Viśvantara is portrayed on this tanka. The progression of scenes is described in the ninth birth-succession story in Chapter II. In the St. Louis series the Viśvantara story is divided: three-quarters of it is shown on Tanka 5; the last quarter is on Tanka 6 along with the tenth birth succession.

story of Ārya Śūra's ruru deer rather than the Jataka of Goldenside, but the two stories are basically the same.)

GELONGS:

In long-passed-away time, a king called Maheśvarasena entered into rulership in Benares, a town rich, happy, prosperous (having good years), filled with beings and with many men. His queen was called Moonlight. Whatever dream she saw, according to all of it there did not happen anything otherwise.

In the country of that king, the Bodhisattva, having been born among the deer, became Lord of the deer. Called Goldenside (*Gser-gyi-glo*), he had a brightness of body beyond the comprehension of human intellect. He was disposed to act in the way of being pleasing to the mind and eye of the whole world. Whoever saw him, that one he examined and remained in that same way (examining). The more he examined, (the more) he turned to doubt, being alarmed and terrified because of fearing hunters and other inhabitants of the world.

This being nature, from the beginning and for a long time afterward, the beasts, too, were able to speak in the words of men. So, then, a raven, having come near that one, being acquainted with him and accustomed to make discourse with him, said, "O mother's brother! Why do you act with such fear and terror?"

"Nephew, because this body of mine, blessed with destiny, produces the whole world's wanting it, I do act with fear of the world and terror of hunters."

"Uncle," said the raven, "because I fear the owl even more than that, we will act to keep guard, one for the other. During the day I will watch over you. At night you watch over me." Thus, having made such promise, those two lived.

One day, a man, his hands securely bound with fetters behind his back, was flung by an enemy into turbulent waves of steeply running water. While being carried away, he cried out loudly his affliction, uttering lamentation in words of compassion:

> "By whom today my life, in this world
>   Difficult to obtain, is given back,
>   As servant acting of him will I be,
>   Even as waiting servant will I act."[3]

By the power of fate, that Lord of the deer, because he was thinking of water, surrounded entirely by herds of deer, had come near the bank of that river. There, having heard the man crying out for help, those deer fled everywhere.

This being nature, although Bodhisattvas have their bodies fallen amiss (that is, in lower than human form) but not their minds, that deer Lord, his heart moistened with compassion, immediately set about to enter that river. The raven, mindful of the promise made earlier with him, wholly keeping guard, following after that one, who knew how to exert himself to draw the man out, said these words to him: "Lord of the deer, come out! Come out! Do not act rashly! These men are ungrateful and do not know it!"

Because the Bodhisattva Great Beings are not to be dissuaded, he (the deer), not listening to that one's words, having (already) entered the river, mounted the man upon his back as a beloved only son and got him out on the bank of the river.

Having unloosed the fetters, after recovering breath but for a moment, he said, "Son, on this way, at your pleasure go!"

That man, then, joining together the palms of his hands, touched the two (front) feet of that leader of the deer and said thus:

> "By you, my life, which is in this world
>   Difficult to obtain, in being given back,
>   O father, subject of you am I,
>   So, even as waiting servant will I act."

By him (the deer) was said:

"Today as servant to me you are not to act,
  Nor even as my waiting-servant.
  But as someone might come and kill me for my skin,
  To any other one you must not show me!

"In short, O son, by you this is to be done. Because the whole world will be attracted to this body of mine and will wish to have it, with your not showing it to anyone you will (thus) be of use (to me) in return for what I have done."

"According to that will I act," that man then promised; and, having circumambulated the Lord of the deer three times, he touched his two (front) feet and went away.

At some time or other, when Queen Moonlight, having become tired from diversion, had duly fallen asleep in her great bed, she saw, in the last watch of the night, a leader of deer, most agreeably formed, sitting on the throne, explaining religion to the many attendants of the king. Having seen it, as it happened in her own personal experience, happiness arose in her from the dreaming of that dream; and, very quickly arising from her bed, she told it to the king.

When the king heard it, the greatest wonder rose up in him concerning the difference of that dream from the truth of it. There took place in him a going toward not liking its sitting on the throne and preaching religion to the many attendants of the king.

Then Moonlight, her way of acting full of joy and praise and luminous discourse—(so that) the king but for a moment (too) rejoiced —said to him: "O Lord, for the sake of finding that deer, I beg you to employ exertion!"

The king, then, ordered his ministers: "O wise ones! The hunters, as many as live in my country, all those summon before me!"

Then the ministers ordered the king's men in the different provinces: "By the Lord has been commanded: 'Bring here the hunters dwelling in my country!' So, when they show themselves, let them all depart for here!''

They (the king's men) having sent out all the hunters dwelling in the provinces to the presence of the king, the ministers brought them before the king.

"O wise ones!" the king addressed them. "In my country there is a leader of deer, exceedingly agreeably formed. As you have heard this from me, that one being soft and tender, take hold of him loosely, and bring him unharmed to me."

"O Lord," they answered, "as to that one's existing, while we were traversing the country of the Lord previously several times also, such an excellent deer we have not heard of, to say nothing of having seen him. O Lord, from one to another was it spoken, 'In such and such a direction he is.' Thus, to us, who listened to them, they had the way of saying it. So, certainly, we will accomplish what the Lord has commanded."

The king then ordered the ministers: "O wise ones! In Benares make proclamation (publish by ringing the bell): 'Listen, wise ones of the crowds of peasants living in Benares and of people coming together from the various regions! By our Lord were these words uttered: "By there being an exceedingly agreeably formed leader of deer in my country, by whom is submitted into my ear news of him, with great respect will I honor him and to him will I give five excellent villages." ' Thus order!"

Then the man who had seen that deer thought, "Shall I act for a little while to keep following the round of transmigration? Or, if not, shall I act to be grateful?" So thinking, holding on to each desire separately in not doing the sinful deed, his heart beaten by the strong fire of hatred (in being) excited by desire for what he did not have, he (further) thought, "For a little while having been grateful, lay it aside! It has come to the time for turning over the stag to the enemy. What state similar to that shall I come to obtain? [He knew that he would certainly be born in a lower form in his next life on earth, presumably as an animal, for this dastardly act of betrayal of the deer.] After a little, I will turn over the stag to him."

The next morning, being within the circle of those taking care of the wants of the king, remaining at the wide doors of the royal palace, bearing all sorts of very sweet-scented flowers, from one to another doorkeeper and minister having passed, he entered within the circle of those being heard by the king. Having first performed manifold gestures of respect, he said to the king: "O Lord, in such and such a direction having gone, in a forest of all sorts of trees, made beautiful with the accustomed birds and animals, there is a deer, called Golden-side, entirely surrounded by many thousands of herds of deer. To the Lord I will show that sacred deer, exceedingly agreeable in form."

When the king heard that, happiness arose in his mind. And, surrounded entirely by many hundreds of thousands of ministers and others, greatly wondering, coming together from the various provinces, also by peasants and countrymen dwelling in Benares placed in front, with that man showing the way, gradually he came to that spot with his followers.

Inasmuch as that raven, being together with the Bodhisattva, was sitting on a tree of the forest thicket, looking in that direction, he saw the great crowds of people coming, turned toward the forest thicket. Swiftly he came to the leader of the deer and said: "O King of the Deer, earlier (I spoke about) your unthinkingly being useful to men, that they are ungrateful and do not perceive it. As I said, so is it. Led by that man, many people are coming. The deer, frightened by the sound of them, have fled everywhere."

The Bodhisattva leader of the deer thought, "If I do not protect these deer today, by its coming to the grinding of my mouth to pieces for that same, rather than that living beings should be annihilated, it is preferable that my own life be consumed." Having thought this, he went to meet the king.

Then that man, without compassion, not seeing the world beyond, his mind diligent (only) on seeing the deer, with both hands pointed out that most excellent of deer and said, "O Lord, this, indeed, is the leader of the deer!"

Exactly at the moment that he said these words, without regard to its being the time of perfect ripening of very violent deeds, entirely at an end, his two hands fell down upon the earth.

With aversion, the king then asked that man, "Hear ye, friend, this, from what has it happened?"

Pained by his affliction, in unclear crying voice, he (the man) said in verses:

"Great King, whoever, having killed,
 Takes wealth away, he is a robber.
 One who ungrateful is, Great King,
 That one, indeed, is robber chief."

The king said, "Hear ye! What is the meaning of that said by the friend?"

Its having turned in such a way, he (the man) told the king everything fully.

Then the king spoke back to that man, a waster of deeds, in verses:

"Why sank you not down into a vile place?
 Your tongue, why was it not cleft into a hundred pieces?
 A body such as yours, rather than kill,
 Why not beat into diamond parts by spear and great arrow?"[4]

The king, then, understanding that great strength of the Bodhisattva, said to his ministers, "O wise ones! This Great Being leader of the deer being worthy of veneration, order the city and the way to it cleared for him!"

Removing the stones, the small stones and gravel of that town, they sprinkled it with sandal water, arranged scented perfuming pans, erected banners, cleansed the many silken ornaments, and scattered all sorts of flowers, making it like the groves of the pleasure-garden of the gods.

Orders having been given to make the way likewise beautiful, crowds of people dwelling in Benares fastened on wreaths of flowers and proceeded to go to meet the Great Being.

Then the king, with great preparation having made enter that exceedingly agreeably formed leader of the deer into the town of Benares, caused him to sit on the throne. And then the king, rich and powerful, surrounded by consorts, youths, and ministers, together with peasants and countrymen, sat down.

The Bodhisattva leader of the deer, then, looking about at the circle, expounded such and such religion to the king and his retinue.

Having heard him, the king and his retinue received the five fundamental laws of the doctrine. Many living beings (thus) obtained the roots of happiness. That forest, then, the king gave to the deer; and to all creature beings, he gave freedom from fear.

"Gelongs, what think you? At that period of time, the leader of the deer, Goldenside, who he was, he indeed I myself was. At that period of time, the man, who he was, he indeed this same Devadatta was. Then this one was ungrateful and did not perceive it. Now, too, this one is ungrateful and does not perceive it. At another time, also, how this Devadatta was ungrateful and did not perceive it, listen!"

In the story that followed, it was as a monkey-chief that the Buddha rescued a wreathmaker who had fallen into a chasm in trying to get mangoes to take back to the king. While the Buddha was resting from his exertion, supposedly guarded by the wreathmaker, that ungrateful man (Devadatta) killed him with a big stone in order to get his flesh to eat, saving the mangoes his rescuer had bestowed upon him to take to the king.

"At another time, also . . . listen!"

The Buddha as a Woodpecker[5]

GELONGS:

In bygone days, the Bodhisattva, remaining (still) in unreal bodily accumulation [that is, not having reached the real or higher-being-body state], was born again among birds, as a woodpecker (female), in an uninhabited solitary mountain region abounding in streams and flowers and fruits. On one side of that same mountain, a lion, king of beasts, behaving and living as he wished, killed deer and ate them. At some time or other, from eating meat, a bone got between his teeth. Although (by nature) free from fear or anxiety, having to put up with the tooth-ache that tormented him, he was unable to eat.

By the power of fate, that woodpecker, accustomed to wander from one tree opening to another, came from the side (where he was) to the side where sat the lord of beasts. Perceiving the lion's distress, seeing him in pain, he (the woodpecker) said, "Uncle, from what have you become suffering?"

"Nephew," [thus in the Tibetan, although the word "woodpecker" is in the feminine form] said the lion, "I am pained from feeling distress."

"Your distress, of what sort is it?"

The lion described it in detail, and the woodpecker said, "Uncle, having examined you, by my being able to be of use to you, you, being a lion and so lord of all four-footed ones, from time to time act to be useful to me!"

"So will I act!" the lion said.

Thought the woodpecker, "Taking care with this one so that he does not notice it, (only after) I have examined and cured him will I then let him know it." So he thought; and applying himself to act to be useful, he sat examining the lion's behavior and posture.

The peak of the malady having passed downward, that lord of

beasts knowing (taking on) a happy humor, went to sleep on a great broad rock, with his jaws opened wide. Then that woodpecker, going up to that king of beasts, seeing him in such an advantageous position, thought, "It has come to the time of treating this one's case."

After carefully examining him, perceiving that a bone had got between his teeth, he (the woodpecker), continually keeping up a fluttering of his wings, at once pulled it out. And the lion, having arisen, with eyes clear from having overcome sleep, remained sitting up.

Then that woodpecker, seeing that that lord of beasts was freed from distress and unhappiness, in great joy went up to him and said, "Uncle, this is the bone that became the cause of your pain."

In great astonishment, that lord of beasts then said, "Nephew, as return to you for this usefulness, I will certainly act to be useful to you. From time to time, come!"

"Good! Thus will I do!" said the woodpecker and (contentedly) went away.

At another time, while the king of beasts was eating meat, that woodpecker, having been seized by a falcon and having (narrowly) escaped death, with eyes tormented by hunger, came near to that lord of beasts and, making known his suffering, said, "Uncle, because of my suffering from hunger, give me a little piece of flesh!"

In verses, the lion replied:

"Now, I am cutting off life;
Fierce am I, not virtuous.
You, who have come between my teeth,
Do you not think remaining alive a great favor?"

The woodpecker also spoke in verses:

"Accumulations fallen down into the ocean,
Thoughts (out of) dreams are without profit.
Without profit are relying upon a bad man
And acting for an ungrateful one."

"Gelongs, what think you? The woodpecker? I. The king of beasts? Devadatta. Then . . . now. . . . How, at another time . . . listen!"

Five more stories followed in the series, each one beginning with "How, at another time . . . listen!," before the Buddha told of the greatest of his former existences, his last earthly life but one. It is the story of Viśvantara, who completely fulfilled the Pāramitā of Giving, first among the six *paramitā*'s held fundamental to the attainment of bodhi. (See Tanka B, Plate XV.)

The Buddha as Viśvantara[6]

GELONGS:

In bygone times a king called Viśvāmitra (Friend of All) entered into rulership in the city of Viśvanāgara, a city rich, extensive, happy, and prosperous, well filled with living beings and with many men; free from brawling and quarreling, from contending and combating, without robbers and thieves; with disease very much abated; and provided with all sorts of desirable things, rice and sugar cane, oxen and buffaloes.

Having entered into his rulership as a religious king, possessed with religion in accordance with the Law, his faith pure, his mind virtuous, he set about being useful to himself and to others, compassionate, striving for Buddhaship, one loving mankind.

At a certain time, he having enjoyed intimacy with his wife in happiness, she became pregnant. Eight or nine months having passed, she brought forth a boy, finely formed, handsome, pleasing to look upon, the color of his skin like gold, his head like a canopy, shoulders long, magnitude of forehead, overhanging eyebrows, the arch of his nose high, limbs and joints all complete.

After his birth, they made a splendid birth feast and proceeded to question how to name the boy. His relatives said, "This boy, being the son of King Viśvāmitra, is therefore to be called Viśvantara (*thams-*

cad-sgrol, deliverer-of-all)." Having named him Viśvantara, they turned him over to eight nurses: two for carrying him, two for suckling him, two for keeping him clean, two for playing with him. Bringing him up on milk and curds, butter and melted butter, the essence of butter, and the most excellent diversities of other necessaries, they made him grow quickly, like a lotus in a pond.

When he became grown, having learned writing, counting, and hand-reckoning, as one of the Kshatriya class consecrated to be a king, one attaining riches and power and might of country, he applied him-self to various spheres of arts and accomplishments, such as these: mounting on the neck of elephants and on horses, carriage practice, handling sword and bow, advancing and retreating, casting with a hook, throwing a noose, discharging large arrows, cutting, cutting open and piercing, seizing, marching, hitting from a distance, renowned hitting, mortally hitting, hitting without escape. These five (?) danger-ous spheres he turned to performing.

The youth Viśvantara, with pure faith and virtuous mind, setting about being useful to himself and others, compassionate, striving for Buddhaship, kindly toward mankind, generously giving, bestowing everything, without attachment entirely renouncing, walked in the path of great giving. Having heard of his excessive giving, people from even a hundred miles away, looking for profit, came to him, all of whom he sent away with the hopes in their minds completely fulfilled.

One day, then, the Bodhisattva entered his chariot, blazing with jewels, and with gold and silver, and diamonds, coral, lapis lazuli, spug [one of the five divine stones], rubies, and sapphires; constructed from the most excellent part of the sandalwood tree; covered with skins of lion, tiger, and leopard cat; drawn by four horses, swift-going like the wind in its power, causing to sound sets of gold and silver bells. And from the holy city early into the park he went.

Then some Brahmans, knowing the Vedas and the branches of the

Vedas, met him and said, "O Kshatriya youth! May you be victorious!,"
also saying:

"You, indeed, All-giving, thus,
In the whole world are perfectly renowned.
Upon the Brahmans, then, this chariot
As gift, fitting it is that you bestow."

With their having said these words, the Bodhisattva Viśvantara
quickly alighted from that chariot and, with cheerful, contented,
greatly rejoicing heart, gave that chariot to the Brahmans, saying:

"As by me with greatest joy
The chariot to the Brahmans has been given,
So by me, the three worlds having been given away,
May be known the highest bodhi!"

At another time, having mounted the most excellent of elephants,
called Rājyavardhana (Government-increasing), having color like unto
jessamine blossoms, white lotus, snow, silver, and white clouds, the
seven (principal parts of the body) duly grown, feet and trunk well
formed, looking haughty and striding along like the son of Airāvana
(Indra's elephant), marked with signs of distinguished gifts regarded
as having come from having performed meritorious actions, he went,
followed by troops of devoted slaves, friends, and attendants, like the
moon surrounded by assemblages of constellations, at time of spring,
into the forest park where trees their flowers were opening, and geese
and cranes, peacocks and parrots, mynas, cuckoos, and pheasants were
calling. Then some Brahmans, incited by an adversary, came quickly
up to the youth Viśvantara and said to him, "O Kshatriya youth! May
you be victorious!," also saying:

"With beings in the world divine and not divine,
You, indeed, All-giver, thus, are famed.

So then this splendid elephant of yours
Fitting it is, to us to give."

With their having said this, the Bodhisattva, quickly alighting from that splendid elephant, with mind cheerful, contented, and greatly rejoicing, gave that best of elephants to them, saying:

"As by me with greatest joy
The elephant to the Brahmans has been given,
So by me, the three worlds having been given away,
May be known the highest bodhi!"

Thus was it heard: "Viśvantara, son of King Viśvāmitra, has given away the splendid elephant, called Rājyavardhana, to some Brahmans, incited by an adversary." King Viśvāmitra, also having heard this, becoming very angry and disturbed, summoned the youth Viśvantara and said: "You, now, take leave of my country! (Without remaining, go!)"

Renounced, then, by his father, the youth Viśvantara thought:

"Because of having made exertion for the sake of bodhi and because of having put on the armor of intentional zeal for the sake of being affected toward the whole world, that elephant even I gave away.

"As long as I dwelt at home, indeed,
I gave as gifts what I was able.
In relying, indeed, on the penance-forest,
There are certainly excellent things to do.
Having been asked, to utter 'I do not give,'
Thus, the words to speak, I cannot say.
Rather than that, renouncing home,
I will into the penance-forest go."

On his heart having thus incised his lofty vow, the Bodhisattva went back to his wife Madrī and told her those things in detail. As soon as Madrī heard him, with heart fearful of being separated from her loved one, she joined together the palms of her hands and said to the Bodhisattva:

"O son of the King! If this be so, I too will go into the penance-forest. Parted from you, indeed, O son of the King, I cannot bear to live even for a moment! Why, if one asks?

"As the sky deserted by the moon,
  As earth of harvest desolated,
  As lotus is, deprived of water,
  So is a wife forsaken by her husband."

Said the Bodhisattva: "Undoubtedly, at the end we shall have come to be separated. This is, indeed, the nature of the world. You, your body being accustomed to excellent food and drink, bedding and clothing, are very happy. In the penance-forest one sleeps on grass and leaves spread on the ground; one eats roots, flowers, and fruits; one walks on ground filled with sward grass, piercing stones, and thorns, relying on one food again and again; one is obliged to habituate oneself to all living beings and to exert oneself in honoring strangers (ones coming suddenly). Even there, undoubtedly, with regard to my giving gifts to the best of my ability, you must not feel even the least regret. Therefore think about this duly a little more."

Madrī replied: "O son of the King, as long as I am able, I will carry out things along with my Lord."

"If so," said the Bodhisattva, "be mindful of the promises you have made."

Then the Bodhisattva went to his father, and, having with his head paid reverence, said:

"O father, the giving of the elephant away by me as a present,
  A fault committed, I beg the Lord of Earth forgive!
  When I from city into wilderness am gone,
  Your treasury, O Lord of Men, empty will not become."[7]

The King, then, losing his voice from affliction at separation from his son, said in tremulous tones: "O son, relinquish the thought of giving and stay here!"

The Bodhisattva replied:

"Earth, together with its mountains even,
 If possibly undergoing change,
 O Lord of Earth, my mind acts not
 In undergoing change from giving."

Thus having said, he went away. Then, with son and daughter and wife, he entered the chariot and went forth from that holy city, followed by men of the palace retinue and country people, wailing, hundreds of thousands of them.

A certain man, having heard the sounds of wailing and lamentation, having also seen the great crowds of people proceeding to the gate of the city, asked another man, "Halloo, friend! This great crowd of people giving forth such lamentation, from what has it happened?"

"O wise one!" was the answer. "Don't you know why? In this way it is: the son of the Lord of Men himself, Sudanta (having beautiful teeth),[8] steadfast in character, rejoicing in great giving, has been banished from here."

When the prince, with his wife and children, had reached the edge of the forest, the palace retinue assembled there raised loud lamenting cries. Then the Bodhisattva, having in some measure gone openly, now said to the palace retinue that had come forth from that holy city:

"Wisdom-possessing ones! Go back! Go back! Even after, in this way, having been held together with loved ones for a very long time, at the end, undoubtedly, separation comes. Relatives and friends undoubtedly become separated from dear ones, as from the trees of the hermitage which put an end to the fatigues of a journey. Why, if one should ask?

"Having reflected that in the whole world,
People, being powerless, become separated from friends,
You, act by all exertions on the earth,
For the sake of peace to hold your minds unmoving!"

When the Bodhissattva had traveled three hundred yojanas, a Brahman, seeing him, came up to him and said, "O Kshatriya youth! Having heard of your virtues, by my having come from a country as much as three hundred miles from here, it is fitting that this excellent chariot of yours should come to me as recompense for my fatigue."

Then Madrī, unbearableness having arisen, with abusive words said to that Brahman:

"Alas! This Brahman, his mind utterly merciless,
Even in the forest asks of the King's son!
The King's son, fallen from his royal splendor!
To him, here, arises not any compassion whatsoever?"[9]

The Bodhisattva said, "Blame not the Brahman! Why, if one should ask?

"Madrī, were there not such as these, riches desiring and accepting,
All-giving then not being, not anyone on earth to bodhi would attain.
By means of giving and the others of the six Pāramitās comprising highest virtue,
The Bodhisattvas to highest all-knowingness attain!"[10]

Then the Bodhisattva, with greatest of rejoicing, gave the carriage with its horses to that Brahman and said:

"May I, O Brahman, acting to remove impurity of avarice
By this excellent gift here of the chariot,
In motion set the great chariot of the Stainless Law
By great and most excellent rishis set in motion!"

Then Viśvantara, with greatly rejoicing mind from having given that best of chariots to the Brahman, set out, carrying the young boy

Krishna on his shoulder, with Madrī, carrying the young girl Jālinī, in the direction of the penance-forest and gradually came to arrive at the penance-forest. In that penance-forest grove, then, Viśvantara dwelt, performing with his own heart's joy the penance exercises he had undertaken.

When (one day) Madrī had gone from the penance-forest for roots and fruits, a Brahman came to Viśvantara and said:

"O Kshatriya youth! May you be victorious!

"To us, because of slave not being,
  Wandering with walking cane I go.
  Your children two, because of that,
  By you to give to me is fitting."

With his having said these words, the Bodhisattva became a little thoughtful about his giving away his beloved children, and the Brahman then said to the Bodhisattva Viśvantara:

"O Kshatriya youth! In my having heard of you as All-giver, so by my having asked of you, what is there to examine about it?

"You, indeed, renowned on the earth
  As having the nature of all-giving compassion,
  In accordance with such renown as that,
  Fitting it is that you constantly act."

With his having said these words, the Bodhisattva Viśvantara said to that Brahman:

"O great Brahman!

"In giving away my own life, even,
  Examining I would not experience at all.
  What then, in giving my children away,
  Is to be said about changing to another mind?

"O great Brahman, in this way it is:
  These children two, brought up by me in the forest

Happily, wholly given away, how these will live
From mother miserably separated, I am thinking of.

"'The youth Viśvantara, without affection
In having given his children, not himself,'
Thus, some will come to blame me.
O Brahman, best is it me to take."

Then the Brahman said to Viśvantara:

"O Kshatriya youth! Born into great royal family, virtue renowned
on this whole earth, toward all beings because of pity, yes, into kindness having entered, with presents and offerings and marks of respect,
like a sweet-scented elephant, honoring sramanas, Brahmans, and
strangers, fulfilling completely the hopes in the minds of all poor and
needy people, unprotected and hungry ones, am not I, you having
seen my purpose in having come, to be satisfied? Tired by the journey, am I not to have recompense? Seeing, profitless, hopes and wishes
for a long time striven and striven for, to be done without recompense, that indeed not being my share, by you to nothing brought?
Your thus-said words, in having hit the horse of completely examining
the hope in my mind, comes to my quickly turning back. Rather than
that, having acted to fulfill completely the hope in my mind, it is
fitting that you give me the children. Why, if one should ask?

"Even one who gave away the earth wearing as clothing its water-treasure,
As matchless eyes its food-fields, the excellent ample mountains
As breasted upper part of body, together with towns and villages,
With you, Sudāna, in being able to give is not equal."

Having heard those words of the Brahman, the Bodhisattva Viśvantara pondered on them because of being caught up in love for the
children:

"If once the two children
To the Brahman I have given,

Affliction rising from the separation
By me and Madrī are obtained.

"But if I do not give them to him,
Failed in exercise of penance have I.
That Brahman, then, his time consumed,
As came he here so goes he back.

"In second place, in torment separated from the children,
Misery on earth is mine to accept.
So, one having not kept my vow,
Failing am I in exercise of penance."

Then the Bodhisattva Viśvantara, having decided that he would
certainly give up his children, said:

"Well, by me,

"By one hundred penances, will be prepared the connecting bridge
For carrying across to the other side ones sinking
Into the measureless depths of the great sea
Of world affliction causing manifold fears."

Face and form like the spotless full moon, his countenance undis-
mayed, having uttered these words, his eyes filled with the moisture
of tears, he gave the two children to that Brahman. Further, he said:

"The fruit of having given these children, indeed,
Has turned to my obtaining the Great Seal.
Thereby shall I save the inhabitants of the world
From the ocean of transmigration."

As soon as he had given away the young children, this earth shook
in six directions. Then, by that earth's having shaken, the penitents
dwelling in that part of the forest spoke back and forth to one another:

"The earth, indeed, become intolerably shaking,
Of whose power is this the sign?
Whose power does this resemble?
Is it very clearly to be made known?"

A certain old penitent there, one of the Vasishṭha lineage, a Master in understanding signs, made the ascetics comprehend, saying: "Undoubtedly, Viśvantara, for the sake of completely saving people suffering from affliction, has given away his two children dwelling in the penance-forest, partaking of fruits and water, agreeable in mind and pleasing to the eye. Therein has the earth become shaken."

Then those two young children, their minds perceiving that their father was really giving them entirely away, weeping cries of compassion, joined the palms of their hands together and, touching the two feet of Viśvantara, said:

> "O father! Without mother's being here,
> Do you wish to give us away?
> After she has come, seeing her a little,
> Then we beg you to give us!"

With affliction laid on his mind, then, the Bodhisattva, filled full, closed up, grieving, with tears flowing down his face, embraced those two and said:

> "O children!

> "In my heart is no unkindness,
> No lack there is of love and of compassion.
> For sake of being useful to the whole world,
> Seeing what virtue is, have I given you away,
> From which my highest bodhi
> And tranquillity, having by self obtained,
> I may save the inhabitants of the world,
> Without support dwelling in the ocean of misery."

Then those two young children, understanding that their father really was entirely giving them away, paid reverence at both feet of their father, and, joining palms of hands together, with cries of lamentation and softly flowing words, said to him:

"If by you the cord has been cut off,
Well, by the two of us, a message:
Act to forgive us, thus (we say).
O father, we beg you to say it!

"O father, furthermore:

"Whatever faults we have committed to you, our superior,
Because of being children, or words said partly unpleasing,
Or wholly willing to obey you with respect, not having done the same,
Knowing them to be the faults of children, act to forgive, we beg!"

Having said these words, they paid reverence to their father, circumambulating him three times, and, with tear-filled eyes, faces toward their superior in way of speaking to him because of impressing him on their minds, looking back again and again, they emerged from that hermitage and went away.

Then the Bodhisattva, his heart contracted by those words of the young children, so fitted for compassion, with his mind offering up a wishing prayer for bodhi, entered the thatched hut of that penance-grove.

No sooner had the children gone away than the great system of the three thousand worlds was shaken in six directions. Many thousands of gods, too, sent forth exclamations of joy and sounds of laughter:

"Oh, excellent giving, the very essence of it
In having given away those two children!
One in whose mind no changing is,
A wonderful one he certainly is!"

Then Madrī, carrying roots and fruits, having set out in the direction of the hermitage, because of the shaking in that great earth plain, all the more quickly went. Some deity or other—having thought "Madrī will come to act as a hindrance of the Pāramitā of giving done by the Bodhisattva in the way of exerting himself to save all living beings"—changed herself into the form of a lioness and stood there barring the way.

Madrī said to that wife of the King of Beasts:

"O wife of the King of Beasts, full of blandishment!
 Why stand you there, barring my way?
 That I be not blamed because of that,
 Step from my way that I go swiftly on!

"Furthermore:

"As you are wife of the King of Beasts
 And I of the lion Lord of Men,
 By being consorts, sisters religious we have become.
 Let the Queen of Beasts, then, make way for me!"

With Madrī's having said these words, the deity who had changed into the form of a lioness went aside from the way.

Then Madrī, having seen unpropitious signs, for a moment thought, "As in the atmospherical space sobbing cries are sounding, and as the creatures living in the grove give forth lament, undoubtedly something not good has arisen in the hermitage." Having reflected, she said:

"As my eye wavers and
 The birds give forth cries,
 As I indeed have feared,
 Those two children have been given away.

"As this earth shakes and
 My heart indeed trembles,
 My body, too, from sickness,
 Those two children have certainly been given away."

A hundred thousand similar unhappy things thus thinking, she went on to the hermitage. Entering it, she looked unhappily about; and, not seeing the two children, despairing and with trembling heart, followed the tracks left on the ground of the hermitage.

(Thus she thought:) "On this side, the youth Krishṇa, together with his sister, always played with the young of the gazelles. This is the house made by those two from the dust of the earth. These, being the playthings of the two, the two not being seen, if they have disappeared unseen by me, is it possible that they have gone into the thatched hut to sleep?" In mind thus, in heart hoping, and wanting to see the children, she placed the roots and fruits at one side, and, with tear-filled eyes having touched the feet of her husband, said: "O son of the King! The boy and the girl, where are they?"

Viśvantara said:

"To me there came a Brahman.
With hope, really, he came.
Those children both I gave to him.
Rejoice at that!"

With his having said these words, she—like a gazelle struck by a poisoned arrow, on the ground struck down; like a fish taken out of its waterplace rolling about; like a crane, its young lost, uttering lamenting cries; like a cow, its calf dead, giving forth all sorts of low sounds—said:

"Faces like young lotuses having,
Hands like lotus arrows,[11] tender-fleshed,
My two children, who did not suffer,
Going wherever they have gone, now suffer.

"Straight like young gazelles, eyed like gazelles,
Together with gazelles the hermitage enjoying,
Today my two children, going in such a way,
By power of others, have come to suffer.

"Their eyes with tears filled full,
Sobbing lament, most sorrowful,
Not duly seen by me today,
Among the poor in misery they live.

"Those two, from mother separated and from near ones,
Rashly by relatives given up,
With sinful men together having come,
My two children are very much afflicted.

"With thirst and hunger constantly tormented,
　The two, undoubtedly becoming slaves of those
　Under whose power they come to go,
　Affliction of complete exhaustion will suffer.

"Surely in other existences here have I
　Committed very sinful deeds, intolerable,
　Of separating hundreds of dear ones,
　That, like a cow without its calf, I utter lamentation.

"By what solemn asseveration I, to all living beings,
　Come continually to have evenness of mind,
　By that asseveration may my two children be,
　From having become slaves, made free!"

Then Madrī, looking upon the trees which had been caused to grow
and tended by those children, standing there in their dense foliage,
with love in her heart embracing them, said:

"With water by the children scooped into small gourd bottles
　From your leaves dripping the drops of water,
　O beautiful trees, you were as if possessed with soul,
　As mother to the children giving milk to drink."

Seeing, further, the young gazelles with whom the children had
been accustomed to play, standing in the hermitage, unhappily, with
words of lamentation, gently she said:

"Who, wishing to look upon their playfellows,
　Make search for signs somewhere on earth impressed,
　These young gazelles, too, wandering,
　Not little otherwise (than theirs) my misery is."

Then, seeing on what way those young children had proceeded,
their tracks on that way interrupted, not going onward straight but
filled with crookedness, far more tormented by affliction, she said:

"As marks of pulling toward (someone) appear,
　And some, in part, from going quickly,

Beating, undoubtedly you drove them,
O most merciless Brahman!

"Throat with shortness of breath and voices hoarse,
Trembling, their pretty lower lips, my children!
Eyes like gazelles looking anxiously about,
With tender feet, how went they toward their ruin?"

Then the Bodhisattva, looking upon that one uttering such lamentation, with these and those words, concerned with transitoriness in manifold enumerations, making her understand, said:

"Because of renown, those children two
I did not give away, nor out of anger;
But for the sake of being useful to all living beings,
Those children, difficult, very, to give, I gave away.

"Most difficult to give up, self and
Wife and children, having given,
As it is done by Mahāsattvas,
One comes to attain the highest bodhi.

"O Madrī! Given to giving, those two children
Difficult to give, for the sake of saving the world I gave.
Self, wife, and children, wealth, too, acting to give,
To me the understanding is of giving everything to all."

Madrī, then, keeping up her spirit, said to the Bodhisattva:

"To you no hindrance will I make,
Do not you change to another mind!
If even me you wish to give,
Without scruple, then, give me!

"Furthermore:

"O Courageous One, having quickly attained
That purpose for the sake of which, not (yet) yours,
You give up what is connected with misery,
Act to save beings from the cycle of existence!"

Then Sakra, Lord of the Devas, having perceived the Bodhisattva's

and Madrī's efforts, exceedingly marvelous and very difficult to carry
out, wholly surrounded by assemblages of the thirty-three (gods), came
from the heavens above to that hermitage, lighting up that forest with
hundreds of great lights, and, remaining in the heavens, said to the
Bodhisattva:

"So, in a world mind-darkened, its understanding bound by heeding evil,
  The noose of the heart, by children bound within, attached to enjoyment,
  You, alone, O Excellent Lord, without attachment, in giving away the
    joy-producing children,
  Certainly without difficulty attain degree of stainless happiness and
    tranquillity."

These words thus having said, Sakra, Lord of the Devas, having
made the Bodhisattva feel joyful, thought, "This one, alone, deprived
of servant, may turn to getting into trouble. Well, I will take Madrī
for myself." With this thought, he changed into the appearance of a
Brahman, went to the Bodhisattva, and said:

"Limbs all beautiful, by husband
  Not blamed, affectionate,
  Praised in family, this sister
  Give to me for slave."

Then Madrī, unbearableness having arisen, said to the Brahman:

"O shameless and desirous one,
  You good-for-nothing Brahman!
  For me—not acting as do you, the prostitute,
  But delighting in the pure Law—do you long?"

Then the Bodhisattva Viśvantara, his heart all taken up with compassion, began to look upon Madrī, and she said to him:

"Misfortune for myself I do not borrow,
  About myself I do not care;
  Alone, how you will live, thus does it come to.
  So do I, on account of you, misfortune borrow."

Then the Bodhisattva said to Madrī:

"For me myself, I seek degree beyond intolerable affliction.
  Here on this earth, O Madrī, must I not lament.
  Untroubled, you, this Brahman follow after,
  I in the hermitage will stay, as do the gazelles."

Having said these words, with mind cheerful and contented, greatly rejoicing, he thought to himself:

"This gift here in the forest
  From me the final gift is.
  This Madrī, even, having wholly given away,
  Wholly without attachment I become."

In his mind having understood, he took Madrī by the hand and said to that Brahman:

"This my dear wife, loving of heart,
  Orders obeying, pleasantly spoken,
  As one of high family comporting herself,
  Receive, most excellent of Brahmans, I beg you!"

When Sudāna had given away his wife because of wishing for bodhi, the earth, like a boat on the water, shook to its boundaries in six directions.

Madrī, then, having come into the power of the Brahman, exhausted by the pain of being separated from husband, son, and daughter, throat sounds stopping huskily from shortness of breath, spoke these words:

"What evil kinds of deeds did I
  In former existences commit,
  That now—like a cow, dead its calf—
  In uninhabited forest I mourn?"

Then Sakra, Lord of the Devas, made disappear his Brahman guise, and, remaining in the appearance of his own nature, said to Madrī:

"O fortunate one, a Brahman I am not nor even a man.
Sakra, I am, of Devas Lord, of the Asuras Conqueror.
Rejoiced am I by your having come to highest conquering.
From me whatever promise you may wish, that here declare!"

Made happy by his words, Madrī then made reverence to Sakra,
saying:

"O thou of the thousand eyes, my children,
From becoming slaves may they be freed
And at their grandsire's even
To arrive be made by the Lord of the Thirty-three!"

On those words having been spoken, the Great Lord entered the
hermitage, went up to the Bodhisattva, and, taking Madrī by the left
hand, said to the Bodhisattva:

"By me to you, this Madrī
For service has been given.
Do not you give her to anyonesoever!
Giving away what has been assigned is blameworthy."

Then Sakra, Lord of the Devas, (caused a delusion to fall upon)
that Brahman who had carried away the boy and the girl, making him
think "I am at another town" when he had gone to that same town
(from which the children had departed with their parents) blindly
setting about to sell those young children. As soon as he was seen by
the ministers, they said to the King:

"O Lord!

"With your grandson Krishṇa
And Jālinī, those two,
A very atrocious Brahman, selling them,
Has come to this excellent city."

When the King heard these words, he indignantly said, "Let the
two young ones appear here quickly!" The ministers sent out word,

and the townspeople came speedily together in the presence of the King. As soon as one of the ministers led the children before the King, and the Ruler of Men saw his grandchildren without clothing exposed to view, bodies filthy and dirty, exactly that, he at once fell from his throne to the ground. The palace retinue, assemblages of ministers, the women even, began to weep. Then the King said to the ministers:

"Whoever in the forest dwelling,
His mind delighting in openly giving,
That bright-eyed one, with wife together,
Be summoned quickly here!"

Then Sakra, Lord of the Devas (having caused the children to be returned to their grandfather), made reverence to the Bodhisattva and went away to his own abode.

Some time afterward, King Viśvāmitra having passed away, Brahmans and ministers, together with townspeople, went to that hermitage and besought the Bodhisattva to come to the city. There they appointed him king. Then King Viśvantara became called Viśvatyāga (All-Renouncer).

After he had given many different kinds of presents to Gelongs and Brahmans, the needy and the poor, friends, relatives, kinsmen, and soldiers, he spoke in verses:

"By striving for bodhi,
To Kshatriyas, Brahmans, Vaiśyas,
Śūdras, Chāṇḍālas, and Pukkasas,
Fearlessly have I given gifts:
Gold and silver, oxen and horses,
And jeweled ear ornaments,
Likewise laboring slaves.
Giving is the most excellent of religious duties.
With mind free of attachment,
By my having given son and daughter completely away,
In this world and the other,
Men come to attain purity."

At the time when King Viśvāmitra had given much wealth to the Brahman Jūjaka (when he was found trying to sell the children and was brought to the king by the ministers)—causing him thus to become greatly increased in riches—favorites, relatives, and friends came to him (the Brahman Jūjaka) and said, "Your wealth and abundance and fortune, excellent whatever they may be, all have depended upon that youth Viśvantara."

"What has the youth Viśvantara done for me?" he asked. "Because of having been born in the highest caste, becoming thus a receiver of gifts, therefore I became fortunate."

"Gelongs, how think you?" the Bhagavant said. "At the time of that period, the youth Viśvantara who he was, that was I. At the time of that period, Jūjaka, who he was, this same Devadatta was. Then this one was ungrateful and did not perceive it. Now also, this one is ungrateful and does not perceive it. Therefore, Gelongs, it is to be taught to be grateful and to be aware of it."

NOTES

Notes

The notation for references to Tibetan scriptures has the following parts: (1) the scripture, e.g., Tanjur; (2) the class of that scripture, e.g., mDo; (3) the number of the volume, e.g., 91; (4) the number of the folio, together with *a* for recto and *b* for verso, and the number of the line, e.g., 148*b*.1. Thus: Tanjur, mDo, 91, fol. 148*b*.1.
Reference to the Upanishads is notated as follows: (1) the Prapāṭhaka number; (2) the Khaṇḍa number; (3) the section number. Thus: 8.1.3.

Preface

1. J. S. Speyer (trans.), Ārya Śūra's *The Jātakamālā or Garland of Birth-Stories*. Translated from the Sanskrit (London: Henry Frowde, 1895), pp. 227-28.
2. Léon Feer. *Analyse du Kandjour et Abrégé des Matières du Tandjour, Recueil des Livres Sacrés du Tibet, par Alexander Csoma, de Körös, Traduite de l'Anglais et Augmenté de Diverses Additions et Remarques*, "Annales du Musée Guimet" (Paris: Ernest Leroux), Vol. II (1881), pp. 131-566.
3. Alexander Csoma, de Körös, *Asiatic Researches*, Vol XX (Calcutta, 1836). Four articles: pp. 41-93, 285-317, 393-552, 553-85.
4. P. Cordier, *Catalogue du Fonds Tibétain de la Bibliothèque Nationale* (Paris: Imprimerie Nationale, Ernest Leroux, 1915), Part III, "Index du Bstan-hgyur," p. 417.

I. Tibetan Art and Teaching

1. L. A. Waddell, *The Buddhism of Tibet or Lamaism* (2nd ed.; Cambridge, England: W. Heffer & Sons, Ltd., 1939), pp. 22-23 with notes.
2. W. Woodville Rockhill, *The Life of the Buddha and the Early History of His Order: Derived from Tibetan Works in the Bkah-hgyur and Bstan-hgyur* (London: Trubner & Co., 1884), pp. 215-16.

3. W. R. S. Ralston, *Tibetan Tales, Derived from Indian Sources.* Translated into English from F. Anton von Schiefner's German translation of the Tibetan of the Kah-gyur. (London: Kegan Paul, Trench, Trubner & Co., Ltd., 1906). Introduction, pp. ix-x.

4. Waddell, *op. cit.*, p. 19, note 3.

5. Giuseppe Tucci, *Tibetan Painted Scrolls* (Rome: La Libreria dello Stato, 1949), Vol. I, pp. 267 ff.

6. H. A. Jäschke, *A Tibetan-English Dictionary* (London: Kegan Paul, Trench, Trubner & Co., Ltd., 1934), p. 228.

7. See George Roerich's *Tibetan Paintings* (Paris: Paul Geuthner, 1925), Introduction, pp. 16-20.

8. The descriptions of figures on this transfer impression are paraphrased from W. Y. Evans-Wentz's *Tibet's Great Yogī Milarepa* (London: Humphrey Milford, 1928), pp. xv-xviii.

9. Tucci, *op. cit.*, Vol. I, pp. 269, 286, 291, 294.

10. Tucci, *op. cit.*, Vol. I, p. 268.

11. F. L. Woodward (trans.), *The Book of the Kindred Sayings: Samyutta Nikāya, or Grouped Suttas* (London: Publishers for Pāli Text Society, Oxford University Press, 1924), Part III, p. 139.

12. Tucci, *op. cit.*, Vol. I, p. 300.

13. Robert Ernest Hume, *The Thirteen Principal Upanishads, Translated from the Sanskrit* (London: Humphrey Milford, 1934), p. 263. Chāndogya Upanishad, 8.1.3.

14. Speyer (trans.), *op. cit.*, p. 1.

15. Associate of British East India Company, Nepal, 1821-43; later Resident to the Court of Nepal. Diplomat and negotiator. Student of natural history, ethnology, and linguistics. See S. Dillon Ripley's *Search for the Spiny Babbler, An Adventure in Nepal* (Boston: Houghton Mifflin Co., 1952), pp. 3 ff.

16. Speyer, *op. cit.*, Introduction, p. xxviii.

17. M. Winternitz, *A History of Indian Literature* (Calcutta, 1939), Vol. II, p. 276.

18. F. Max Müller (ed.), *Ārya Śūra's The Jātakamālā or Garland of Birth-Stories* (London: Henry Frowde, 1895), Preface, p. xvi.

19. Waddell, *op. cit.*, pp. 9-12.

20. George N. Roerich (trans.), *The Blue Annals, the Stages of the Appearance of the Doctrine and Preachers in the Land of Tibet* (2 parts; Bengal: Royal Asiatic Society, 1949), Part I, p. 25. Composed by 'Gos lo-tsā-ba gZhon-nu-dpal, A.D. 1392-1481.

21. D. R. Shackleton Bailey, *The Śatapañcāśatka of Mātṛceṭa.* Sanskrit text, Tibetan translation and commentary, and Chinese translation; with an In-

troduction, English translation, and notes (Cambridge: University Press, 1951). Introduction, p. 1.

22. Tanjur, Narthang ed.: mDo, 91, fol. 1*a*.

23. *The Blue Annals*, Part I, pp. 268-69.

24. *Ibid.*, Part II, pp. 1052-54.

25. *Ibid.*, Part II, pp. 532-36.

26. *Ibid.*, Part II, pp. 635-37.

27. *Ibid.*, Part II, pp. 805-37.

28. Jäschke, *op. cit.*, p. 54.

29. *The Blue Annals*, Part II, pp. 805-37.

30. Alfred Foucher, *The Beginnings of Buddhist Art* (Paris: Paul Geuthner, 1917), p. 35. Translated by L. A. Thomas and F. W. Thomas.

31. W. Y. Evans-Wentz, *The Tibetan Book of the Dead, or the After-Death Experience on the Bardo Plane, According to Lāma Kazi Dawa-Samdup's English Rendering* (London: Oxford University Press, 1936), p. 234.

32. E. B. Cowell (ed.), *The Jātaka or Stories of the Buddha's Former Births*, translated from the Pali by various hands (6 vols.; Cambridge: University Press, 1895), Vol. I, Preface, p. v.

33. A. C. Burnell and E. W. Hopkins, *The Ordinances of Manu, Translated from the Sanskrit* (London: Trubner & Co., 1884), p. 96.

34. Evans-Wentz, *The Tibetan Book of the Dead*, Introduction, pp. 49-53. See also B. Jowett, *The Dialogues of Plato* (London: Macmillan and Co., 1875), Vol. III, *The Republic*, Book X, secs. 614-20.

35. G. Gurdjieff, *All and Everything* (New York: Harcourt, Brace & Company, 1950), pp. 763-67.

II. Stories of Scenes on the Tankas

1. Mrs. Rhys Davids, *Buddhism, A Study of the Buddhist Norm* (New York: Henry Holt & Co., undated), p. 10.

2. Müller (ed.), *op. cit.*, Preface, p. xvi.

3. Slightly varying versions of this story appear in R. Spence Hardy, *A Manual of Budhism in Its Modern Development*, translated from Singhalese MSS (London: Partridge and Oakey, 1853), pp. 91-92; Édouard Chavannes, *Cinq Cents Contes et Apologues Extraits du Tripiṭaka Chinois et Traduits en Français* (Paris: Ernest Leroux, 1940), 4 vols., Vol. 1, No. 4, pp. 15-17; Kshemendra, *Avadānakalpalatā*, Tanjur, mDo, Vol. 93, No. 95 (a summary, in English, of the stories in this volume appears in Tucci, *op. cit.* Vol. II, pp. 492 and 528). A very different version of this story appears in two places in the Kanjur: in the *Dzanglun* and in the *Suvarṇaprabhāsottamasūtra*.

4. Pali, No. 499. Also Chariyā-piṭaka, a series of 35 metrical tales based on similar narratives in the Pali-Jataka book, translated by the Rev. D. J. Gogerly, "Buddhism—Chariyā-Piṭaka," *Journal of the Ceylon Branch of the Royal Asiatic Society*, Vol. II, 1848-55 (after p. 354), new paging 5-6.

5. Pali, No. 415.

6. Pali, No. 40

7. Pali, No. 340.

8. Pali, No. 316. Also Chavannes, *op. cit.*, Vol. I, No. 21, pp. 75 ff., and No. 139, pp. 411 ff.; Kshemendra, *op. cit.*, No. 104, translated by Tucci, *op. cit.*, Vol. II, No. 104, pp. 531-32 (very different); the Rev. Richard Morris (ed.), *Buddhavamsa and the Chariyā-piṭaka* (London: Henry Frowde, 1882), Part I, No. 10; Gogerly, *op. cit.*, pp. 10-11.

9. Pali, No. 480. Also Chariyā-piṭaka, *cit.*, I, 1.

10. Pali, No. 547; Waddell, *op. cit.*, pp. 541-43; Hardy, *op. cit.*, pp. 116-24; Chariyā-piṭaka, *cit.*, I, 9; Ralston, *op. cit.*, pp. 257-72; Kshemendra, *op. cit.*, No. 24, and Tucci, *op. cit.*, Vol. II, p. 469; Gogerly, *op. cit.*, pp. 6-10; Jacques Bacot and H. I. Woolf, *Three Tibetan Mysteries*, translated from the French version of the Tibetan by Bacot, *Asiatic Journal*, Sept.-Oct. 1914 (London: George Routledge & Sons, Ltd., undated), "Tchrimekundan," pp. 1-115.

11. Waddell, *op. cit.*, pp. 543-51.

12. Pali, No. 50.

13. Pali, No. 305. The Pali story gives a better account of the old teacher's testing.

14. Pali, No. 527.

15. Pali, No. 463.

16. Pali, No. 75. Also Chariyā-piṭaka, *cit.*, III, 10.

17. Pali, No. 35. Also Chariyā-piṭaka, *cit.*, III, 9; T. W. Rhys David (trans.), *Buddhist Birth Stories or Jātaka Tales*, The Oldest Collection of Folk-lore Extant, Being the *Jātakatthavaṇṇana* (London: Trubner, 1880), Vaṭṭaka Jātaka, pp. 302-6.

18. Pali, No. 512.

19. Very much like the beginning of *The Story of Sumedha*, translated by T. W. Rhys Davids, revised by Mrs. Rhys Davids (London: Routledge & Sons, Ltd. undated), pp. 82-88.

20. Pali, No. 488. Also Chariyā-piṭaka, *cit.*, III, 4.

21. Pali, No. 171.

22. Pali, No. 443. Also Chariyā-piṭaka, *cit.*, II, 4.

23. Pali, No. 533.

24. Pali, No. 528.

25. Pali, No. 516.

26. Pali, No. 483.
27. Pali, No. 482. Also Chariyā-piṭaka, *cit.*, II, 6; Chavannes, *op. cit.*, Vol. I, No. 58, pp. 220 ff.; Kanjur, translated in full in Chapter V.
28. Pali, No. 407. Also Chavannes, *op. cit.*, Vol. I, No. 56, pp. 216 ff.
29. Pali, No. 313. Also Chavannes, *op. cit.*, Vol. I, No. 44, pp. 161 ff.; Kshemendra, *op. cit.*, No. 39, and Tucci (trans.) *op. cit.*, pp. 480-81.
30. Cf. Kshemendra-Tucci, *op. cit.*, No. 96, p. 528.
31. Pali, No. 537. Also Chariyā-piṭaka, *cit.*, III, 12.
32. Pali, No. 510. Also Chariyā-piṭaka, *cit.*, III, 3.
33. Pali, No. 278. Also Chariyā-piṭaka, *cit.*, II, 5; Chavannes, *op. cit.*, Vol. III, No. 432, pp. 187 ff.
34. Pali, No. 308. Also Chavannes, Vol. I, No. 51, pp. 193 ff.; Ralston, *op. cit.*, pp. 311-12; Kanjur, translated in full in Chapter V.

III. Tibetan Scriptures: The Kanjur and the Tanjur

1. W. Y. Evans-Wentz, *Tibetan Yoga and Secret Doctrines* (London: Oxford University Press, 1935), pp. 9-10.
2. Waddell, *op. cit.*, p. 10.
3. The explanation of the seven divisions of the Kanjur is paraphrased from *The Buddhism of Tibet* (pages 159-64), by L. A. Waddell, who got it from Alexander Csoma's analysis.
4. Feer, *op. cit.*, p. 353.
5. See W. Woodville Rockhill, *op. cit.*, pp. 148-62.
6. John Dowson, *A Classical Dictionary of Hindu Mythology and Religion, Geography, History, and Literature* (London: Routledge & Kegan Paul Ltd., 1950), pp. 26-27.
7. Waddell, *op. cit.*, p. 12.
8. Kenneth K. S. Ch'en, "The Tibetan Tripitaka," *Harvard Journal of Asiatic Studies* (Harvard-Yenching Institute, Cambridge, Mass.), June 1946, pp. 53-54.
9. Ch'en, *op. cit.*, p. 56 and note 10.
10. Waddell, *op. cit.*, pp. 262-64.
11. Wesley E. Needham, "The Significance of the Yale Kanjur," *The Yale University Library Gazette* (New Haven, Conn.), July 1952, pp. 48-51.
12. See Eugene Pander, *Das Pantheon des Tschangtscha Hutuktu* (Berlin: Veröffentlichungen aus dem Königlichen Museum für Volkskunde, 1890), Vol. I, Parts 2 and 3, Leaf 93, p. 102. Illustration No. 277 in this book is a picture of Indra in his place in a pantheon of Lamaism—the same image as the Indra seen on the right end of the first leaf of the Suvarṇa-sūtra.

13. Alice Getty, *The Gods of Northern Buddhism* (Oxford: At the Clarendon Press, 1928), p. 166.

IV. Feeding the Tigress

1. See R. Spence Hardy, *A Manual of Budhism in its Modern Development*, translated from Singhalese MSS (London: Partridge and Oakey, 1853), pp. 91-92.
2. Speyer, *op. cit.*, Introduction, p. xxviii, with footnote.
3. Léon Feer, "Le Bodhisattva et la Famille de Tigres," *Journal Asiatique* (Sept.-Oct., 1899), pp. 272-303.
4. Kanjur, Lhasa ed.: mDo, 28, fols. 222*b*.3 to 227*a*.1.
5. Kanjur, Lhasa ed.: rGyud, 11, fols. 192*b*.7 to 206*b*.4.
6. Tanjur, Narthang ed.: mDo, 91, fols. 1-148*b*.1.
7. Tanjur, Peking ed.: mDo, 93, fols. 1-361*a*.8.
8. Speyer, *op. cit.*, p. 2.
9. Lhasa edition: "examining the character (*ts'ul*, instead of *ts'al*, grove) of his former speaking."
10. Lhasa edition: "he went to feed the hungry tigress."
11. Lhasa edition: "Why for the sake only of me (*bdag*)?"
12. Kanjur, Lhasa ed.: rGyud, 11, fols. 192*b*.7 to 206*b*.4.
13. Charity (*dāna*); keeping the precepts (*śīla*); patience under insult (*kshānti*); zeal and progress (*vīrya*); meditation (*dhyāna*); wisdom (*prajñā*). As given in *The Huang Po Doctrine of Universal Mind*, translated into English by Chu Ch'an (London: The Buddhist Society, 1947).
14. See Johannes Nobel, *Suvarṇaprabhāsottamasūtra, Das Goldglanz-Sūtra, Die Tibetischen Übersetzungen mit einem Wörterbuch* (Leiden, Netherlands: E. J. Brill, 1944), pp. 154-74.
15. Feer, "Le Bodhisattva et la Famille de Tigres," *loc. cit.*, pp. 272-303.
16. Thomas Watters, *On Yuan Chwang's Travels in India, 629-645 A.D.* (London: Royal Asiatic Society, 1904), Vol. I, pp. 253-56.
17. G. Ecke and P. Demiéville, *The Twin Pagodas of Zayton* (Cambridge, Mass.: Harvard University Press, 1935), pp. 3-6.

V. Three Jatakas from the Kanjur

1. Hardy, *op. cit.*, pp. 200-20.
2. Kanjur, Narthang ed.: 'Dul-ba, 4, fols. 278*b*.7 to 283*b*.1. Lhasa ed.: 'Dul-ba, 4, fols. 253*a*.6 to 257*b*.4.

3. Seven-syllable verse.
4. Nine-syllable verse.
5. Kanjur, Narthang ed.: 'Dul-ba, 4, fols. 285a.4 to 286b.2. Lhasa ed.: 'Dul-ba, 4, fols. 259a.6 to 260b.3.
6. Kanjur, Narthang ed.: 'Dul-ba, 4, fols. 301b.5 to 314b.7. Lhasa ed.: 'Dul-ba, 4, fols. 274b.4 to 286b.2.
7. Nine-syllable verse.
8. Incorrect Tibetan translation for Sudāna ("having good gifts"), a second name of Viśvantara.
9. Eleven-syllable verse.
10. Thirteen-syllable verse.
11. Young lotus leaves, arrowlike in appearance.

Text type: Linotype Janson
Display type: Monotype Caslon 337 and American Type Founders Georgian Initials
Type composition: Slugs Composition Company
Presswork of text and binding: Haddon Craftsmen
Black-and-white illustrations: Printed in collotype by Meriden Gravure
Frontispiece and jacket: Printed by Civic Printing Company
Paper: Strathmore Fairfield
Format: Designed by Sidney Solomon